BESSIE MAE MAC GENERATIONAL COOKBOOK

Delicious Southern recipes like...
Old Fashioned Bean Pie
Watermelon Rind Pie
Coffee Batter Fried Chicken
and more

DISCLAIMER

Last updated November 12, 2020

The information provided by Bessie Mae Mac Generational Cookbook is for general informational purposes only. All information contained in the cookbook is provided in good faith, however we make no representation or warranty of any kind, express or implied, regarding the accuracy, adequacy, validity, reliability, availability or completeness of any information contained in this book. UNDER NO CIRCUMSTANCES SHALL WE HAVE ANY LIABILITY TO YOU FOR ANY LOSS OR DAMAGE OF ANY KIND INCURRED AS A RESULT OF THE USE OF THE RECIPES/METHODS/PROCEDURES OR RELIANCE ON ANY INFORMATION PROVIDED IN THE BOOK. YOUR USE OF THIS BOOK AND YOUR RELIANCE ON ANY INFORMATION IN THIS BOOK IS SOLELY AT YOUR OWN RISK.

PROFESSIONAL DISCLAIMER

This cookbook cannot and does not contain professional food industry advice. The recipes provided is for general home cooks informational and educational purposes only and is not a substitute for professional advice. Accordingly, before taking any actions based upon such information, we encourage you to consult with the appropriate professional. We do not provide any professional food industry advice. THE USE OR RELIANCE OF ANY INFORMATION CONTAINED IN THIS BOOK IS SOLELY AT YOUR OWN RISK.

INTRODUCTION

We believe the basis for a good product is a good start. We are believers in home grown herbs and vegetables. While producing these herbs and vegetables, there is no doubt of what you are getting in terms of wholesomeness and quality. And you can do it with a home-grown garden or right from your windowsill. The advantages with a garden are three-fold - you will get an extremely good work out by exercising, healthy eating, and total satisfaction in seeing an extremely beautiful nutritious product come into fruition. We shall introduce ways and means of cultivating a garden and making sausage from poultry, beef, lamb, game, or the meat of your choice. American Southern folk home cooking is a long-forgotten art. It has become a welcome task to prepare delicious nutritious foods starting with that age-old adage waste not want not. When it comes to food, we want the absolute best for our family. Planning and shopping are the prerequisites in trimming the fat from your grocery bill and making use of every edible portion and all the while cooking food from scratch at home which is healthy, enjoyable, and frugal as well. Generations before the advent of foods filled with herbicides and pesticides Americans consumed healthier meals and the food was more palatable than it is now. As an adolescent I remember going to the market in the produce section you would find harmless worms emanating from the fruits and vegetables, it stands to reason with rational thought the produce was free from chemical radicals. In this book you will learn to supply your garden with insects that cultivates, such as: the ladybug, lacewings, and nematodes; they are the good guys, and they will protect your garden from Hundreds of renegade insects. However, with this humble work we shall endeavor to bring to people around the Globe exciting food recipes at the breakfast, dinner, and supper table that is very delicious from the southern American folk culture while learning to not waste anything that's edible and with a desire to please yourself, family, and friends you shall become innovative, creative and well loved. Southern folk cooking has seen an era where Grandparents and Parents were teaching their children the art of cooking right from their country kitchen and family organic garden. However, as time has come a plethora of restaurants have dotted the American landscape with a culture of food from various ethnicities that introduced foods from their beloved countries. Thus, the American people have become infatuated with recipes from abroad. Its apropos that people are returning to southern folk home cooking substantiating a REASON for the SEASON consulting those old farmers almanac's for timely planting with a desire to grow and eat your very own nutritious foods right from the family garden. We have tried to create recipes from around the globe for the community of humanity to enjoy their traditional foods with a southern folk twist and touch.

ACKNOWLEDGEMENTS

I am humbly and appreciative of what my beloved MOM Bessie McPeters taught me in the kitchen of our home. My Aunt Mauzia McPeters was the CEO of an enterprising home catering business that served delicious pies and cakes to various organizations, basically she catered from the wholesale perspective. My Aunt Gertha Lee Forms was a contributor of the preparation of food. I also remember Aunt Ellen Ellerbee in 1953 sharing knowledge of experiences in home cooking, extracting wild herbs; blueberries and vegetables; Polk salad, right from the field adjacent to her home that sat just 100 yards from the waterfront that were plentiful with willow and base wood trees used for food and folk medicine, mind you she was a robust 105 years young, Affectionately called sweet Aunt Ellen, she was devout with folk knowledge using herbs (fennel bulbs); for flatulence, (willow bark) for pain. Rosemary in ancient times was a symbol for good memory faculties and in folk medicine it is used as a tonic, as a stimulant to induce vitality. In most every southern city in their yards there were vegetable gardens; with very tall trellises to support vines of the vegetables; tomatoes, okra, collard greens, carrots, and corn, and fruit trees such as banana, apple, peach, grapefruit, plum, orange, lemon, and pomegranate. Hence this generational cookbook has evolved from the fond memories of generations gone by and perhaps we shall see a new expression and love for home grown foods and folk medicine right from the family garden.

FOOD PREPARATION

There are a variety of techniques used for preparing food: BOILING, BROILING; BRAISING, SUBMERGING, OR BLANCHING, GRILLING, ROASTING, SMOKING, BARBECUING. Initially the product must be clean or washed thoroughly in cold water. When after washing food be sure to clean all surfaces with Disinfectants to guard against airborne diseases. The following is the preparation methods used in foods. Boiling; submerging foods in hot rolling water at temperatures of 212 ° F or 100 ° C. Braising: foods are browned in hot fat then submerged in one-eighth of a tasty favorable soup base liquid, transferred to a pan and tightly covered and slowly cooked in an oven. Blanching: abruptly and partially cooking food submerged in hot fat or water for (example) to loosen the skin on tomatoes, peaches, stop the cooking process by submerging food in cold water. Grilling: foods cooked from a source emanating from a source beneath the surface of the food that is being prepared the heat source can be generated by wood, coals, gas, or electricity. Roasting can be done over an open fire or by the dry heat method in a closed oven, usually supplied with vegetables, meats, poultry, and fish. The varied application of smoking meats depends on the creativity of the chef or cook. Smoking food can be accomplished by fashioning an old refrigerator into a smoke house and constructing a container for the wood or coals whereby the smoke from the container emanates into the boxed refrigerator with a temperature gauge fixed on the box. Simmering: submerging food into a hot liquid at the boiling point and thereafter reducing the heat just below 212 °F and keeping the heat to a low simmering mode.

POULTRY

ALMOND DUCK W/ ROASTED BRUSSELS SPROUTS

Four pound duckling
Four cups Brussels sprouts sliced in half
One cup chopped onions
Two cups sliced almonds
¼ cup Bemjag seasonings (recipe page 76)
¼ cup Almond extract

Preheat oven to 350 ° F. Place duckling on a clean work surface. Rub with one tablespoon of extract, seasoning, garlic, and onion. Saturate duckling and sprouts with above ingredients well. Place the sprouts in a medium skillet and roast on top rack for 20 minutes. Remove from the oven and add almonds. Choose two jumbo paper clips and insert around the ankles of duckling. Hang upright in the preheated oven. Slide a baking pan to catch the fat drippings. Roast in the oven for 3 ½ hours. Add the remaining extract to the sprout. The nutty flavor for the sprouts and duck is so good, you cannot duck it!

CHICKEN NIGELLA

Eight pieces of chicken breasts
Two cups chicken stock
One medium onion diced
Two garlic cloves crushed
One bay leaf
One teaspoon of thyme
One teaspoon of white pepper
¼ teaspoon nutmeg 1 cup white grape juice
½ cup butter
One cup heavy cream
¼ cup Nigella seeds
¼ cup flour

Preheat a medium size skillet. Melt half of the butter. Sear chicken for 5 minutes total. Reduce heat and cook chicken on low for 20 minutes. In a separate pan, melt the remaining butter and add onions. Cook until they are translucent. Sprinkle flour over the chicken liberally to make a roux. Deglaze the pan with the white grape juice. Add the cooked onions to the chicken. Make a packet with the vegetables by tying them up in cheesecloth. Add the packet to a pot of boiling chicken stock. Remove the chicken from the pan. Strain the stock with cheese cloth and china cap. Place the chicken in a clean pan. Add the roux, nigella seeds, stock, and cream to the chicken. Bring to a boil and then simmer for about 35 minutes. Sprinkle the nutmeg over to yield a perfect sauce.

*Nigella (common name: black seed) can be bought at any Middle Eastern supermarket.

COFFEE BATTERED FRIED CHICKEN

1 whole chicken cut in 8 pieces
1 pint of coffee strongly brewed
2 quarts vegetable oil
½ cup chicken stock
2 cups flour
1 egg beaten
¼ cup buttermilk
1 tablespoon baking powder
1 teaspoon white pepper
Salt (optional)

Preheat the oil in a large sauce pot to 375 °F. Mix the dry ingredients in a large bowl. Set aside. Mix the liquids into a smooth mixture. Dredge each piece of chicken in dry seasoned flour; dip each piece of chicken in batter. Fry the chicken until golden brown.

ARTICHOKES HEARTS TURKEY CHEESE MELTS

Sixteen slices of cheddar cheese
Four tablespoon mustard
Two teaspoons of smoked spice mix
Eight slices of turkey breast about 1/8 inch
Ten slices of whole wheat bread or white bread.
One pound of cooked artichoke hearts (drained)
One cup of lite mayonnaise
½ cup of chopped basil
¼ cup olive oil

Sauté turkey breast in saucepan with oil and smoked seasoning. Brush cheese and turkey with smoked seasoning then transfer to a broiler. Cook until the cheese is melted. Remove from broiler and brush bread with mustard and mayonnaise. Serve with radish leaves and baby spinach and blue cheese dressing.
Reminiscent of old schooled sandwiches piled high.

SAUTEED PINEAPPLE CHICKEN

One whole chicken (cut in eight pieces)
½ medium pineapple (sliced and diced)
¼ cup grapeseed oil
¼ cup butter
¼ cup honey or brown sugar
White pepper... (Optional)
Salt ... (Optional)

Place butter and oil in saucepan. Add the chicken, pineapple, butter, sugar, and pepper to the pan. Simmer for 45 minutes. Add salt if desired.

SAUTEED CHICKEN BREAST W/ RICE

Two chicken breasts sliced one-eighth inch-thick
One tablespoon cumin
1/8 cup cardamom
Two pounds of long grain rice

Add rice to sauce pot and cover with chicken stock, one-eighth inch above
the level of rice. Bring to a boil and reduce heat. Simmer for about 35
minutes. Sprinkle the seasonings onto the chicken breast. Add chicken
breast to saucepan with oil. Simmer for an additional 20 minutes. Serve
with the cooked rice.

TURKEY W/ GRAVY OLE FASHIONED WAY

Sixteen pound young turkey
Two cups Joanna Marie mixture (recipe page 77)
One gallon chicken stock
Giblets, heart neck and gizzard
2/3 cup flour
Sixteen ounces butter
¼ cup cream
3 ½ cups baste sauce, recipe to follow

Baste Sauce:
Add 2 ½ cups of chicken stock to one cup light butter for baste sauce, simmer and set aside.

In a cast iron skillet add butter, flour and chicken stock to make a roux, let stand. In a separate saucepan, render 4 ounces of butter and Joanna Marie mix. Sauté until the onions are translucent and the Joanna Marie mix is tender. Remove from heat. mashed and strain the mixture. Place turkey in 6gallon stock pot. Add the chicken stock, neck, heart, gizzard. boil for 90 minutes. remove turkey and render to a pan. Place the pan into a preheated 350° F oven. Baste often at intervals of 10 minutes until done, approximately 2 hours. In a skillet, transfer the prepared roux, strained Joanna Marie mixture, heart, neck, and gizzard. Dice and mince and add to a saucepan. Combine roux, chicken stock and cream, making a nice smooth gravy. You may use the above Joanna Marie mix leftovers for the cornbread dressing recipe on page 60.

SMOTHERED CHICKEN W/ SKILLET GRAVY

One whole chicken cut in eight pieces skin removed
½ teaspoon cardamom
One teaspoon marjoram
One teaspoon sage
¾ teaspoon thyme
One teaspoon rosemary
¼ cup olive oil
One pat butter

One teaspoon brown sugar
¼ cup flour
Two cups chicken stock
Salt, pepper (Optional)

In a large skillet add olive oil and butter. place chicken, meaty side up.
Cook for seven minutes. Flip and add flour and spices. flip again and cook
for seven minutes on the flipped side. Add chicken stock, simmer for ten
additional minutes or until gravy is bubbly.

ROASTED QUAIL W/ BACON

Six whole quails
Twelve slices of bacon, any variety
One tablespoon olive oil
½ pound long grain rice
1 ½ quart chicken stock
One tablespoon of butter
Two tablespoons minced shallots
Three cloves of garlic
Salt and pepper to taste

Quail meat is very thin; therefore, it is beneficial to wrap them in bacon or
fat to compensate for the lack of fat on the bird. In a medium saucepan add
rice and chicken stock one inch above the level of rice. Start by cooking on
high heat for seven minutes. reduce heat to a low simmer for 25 minutes.
In a blender add butter, garlic, shallots, olive oil and one cup of stock.
blend to a liquid consistency. In a roasting pan, render quail wrapped in
bacon. Place into an oven preheated to 300° F. Baste using the blended
butter mixture at intervals of every 3 minutes for 20 minutes. Quail is done
once it reaches an internal temperature of 170 ° F.

CHICKEN & MUSHROOMS

Six pieces chicken
Two cups mushrooms sliced
One medium onion diced
One cup cilantro dried
Two tablespoon parsley dried
Two tomatoes peel and seeded cut in ¼ inch pieces.
One tablespoon olive oil
¼ cup butter
One quart chicken stock
One cup white grape juice

Cut chicken into sixteen pieces. Remove the skin and sprinkle with flour.
Season it with salt and pepper (optional). In a cast iron skillet brown
chicken all over in butter and olive oil. Add the cilantro, parsley, grape
juice and chicken stock. Simmer until gravy becomes smooth. Add
tomatoes and mushrooms. Cover saucepan and simmer until tender.
Remove from heat and serve.

HALAL ROASTED CAPON

Eight pound capon
Two cups lemon juice
¼ cup thyme
¼ cup sage
¼ cup annatto
¼ cup marjoram

Place lemon juice and seasonings into container large enough to marinate
the bird. Refrigerate overnight. Preheat oven to 275 ° F. Place bird into
roasting pan with a tight-fitting lid. Cook for four hours or until tender.

SAUTEED PAPAYA CHICKEN BREAST

Two chicken breasts, sliced one-eighth inch thick
Two cloves of garlic minced
¼ cup olive oil
Three shallots
¼ teaspoon cinnamon
¼ teaspoon cardamom
One teaspoon white pepper
Two teaspoons brown sugar
One cup Joanna Marie mix (recipe page 77)
Salt ... (Optional)

Place oil in saucepan. Add garlic and Joanna Marie mix. Combine all ingredients with chicken breast. Place chicken breast in hot oiled saucepan add all spices. Simmer for 30 minutes.

BEST SMOKED CHICKEN

Four whole chickens
Three cups carrots
Three cups mushrooms
Three cups celery
One cup onion, coarsely chopped
Two cups of chicken stock
One cup flour
¼ cup Bemjag seasoning (recipe page 76)
¼ cup cold smoked seasoning (recipe page 76)
Pecan wood for smoker

Mix seasonings together and rub onto the outside and cavity of chickens, set aside. In a mixing bowl add the vegetables, stock, and flour. Mix to form a ball. Divide into four balls and place inside the chicken. Wrap in foil and place in 150 °F smoker for 3-4 hours. Check internal temperature for doneness.

SOUPS & STEWS

COCONUT CHICKEN SOUP

One medium chicken breast cubed ¼ inch
One medium onion chopped
Four cloves garlic
One tablespoon olive oil
One tablespoon sage
½ gallon chicken stock
½ cup shredded coconut
One cup coconut milk
Salt and pepper (Optional)

Pour chicken stock in medium saucepot with olive oil, onions, garlic and spices. Add chicken, coconut and milk. Simmer for 35 minutes.

SOUTHERN BEEF STEW W/ A HINT OF COFFEE

Four pounds of chuck beef cut one-eighth cube
One gallon vegetable broth
One pint brewed coffee your way
Two cups Joanna Marie mix (recipe page 77)
2/3 cup flour
¼ cup olive oil
One teaspoon chili powder
One teaspoon ginger
One teaspoon cardamom

Place olive oil in a large saucepot. Add beef and sear on all sides. Add flour and continue to mix until flour is smooth and creamy. Add Joanna Marie and mix well. Add the vegetable broth, coffee, and dry ingredients. Cook on high heat for 90 minutes. Reduce heat and simmer 5 minutes.

LAMB VEGETABLE STEW

Four pounds meat from shank of lamb cut in cubes
One pound's green bean cut in quarter pieces
½ pounds carrots
One pounds of white potatoes
½ pounds celery
½ pounds broccoli spears
One small red bell pepper
Two teaspoon cardamom
Two teaspoons paprika
Three quarts of chicken stock
¼ cup organic white flour

In a saucepan, add flour to oil to make a roux. In a medium sauce pot bring lamb and stock to a rolling boil. Cook on high heat for 80 minutes. Render roux in sauce pot with lamb. Cook for 10 minutes. Add vegetables and turn off heat. Let stand until serving time.

VEGAN PEA SOUP

Two cups shelling peas…organic or conventional
Two cups snow peas…. organic or conventional
One quart vegetable stock
Two cups of boiling water
Three leek ribs
One sweet onion minced
One tablespoon cold smoke seasoning
One teaspoon peppercorns, freshly ground
Salt (Optional)

Render peas, leeks and onion in a medium sauce pot. Pour boiling hot water into the pot. After a few minutes reduce heat and add the remaining ingredients. Simmer for 30 minutes. Serve with black bread.

ON THE BRAZOS CREAM SOUP

Four medium ears of corn
½ gallon chicken stock
Three egg yolks
½ cup heavy cream
½ cup milk
¼ cup flour
One tablespoon olive oil

Cook corn in boiling water for 5 minutes. Cool corn and cut kernels. Set aside. Make a roux from flour and olive oil. Heat the chicken stock. Beat yolks and add cream and milk. Slowly add this mixture and the roux to the hot chicken stock. Now add the corn and mix well. Simmer for 20 minutes.

BESSIE MAE'S GUMBO

Two chicken breasts, cubed
One cup okra
Three tablespoons Gumbo file spice
Two tablespoon brown sugar
Two tablespoons cilantros
½ gallon chicken stock
Six pounds of shrimp
Two fillet fish diced
One medium onion diced
Three large tomatoes diced
Three cloves garlic
¼ cup flour
One link sausage sliced one-eighth inch thick

Make a liquid roux from flour and chicken stock, set aside. In a medium pot render chicken stock garlic, cilantro, tomatoes, Gumbo file, brown sugar, cayenne, and salt (optional). Bring to a boil reduce heat. Add chicken breast, fish, sausage, and okra. Add roux, simmer for 20 minutes. Serve over rice.

COUNTRY STYLE RABBIT STEW

One 2 pound rabbit cut in thirty pieces
One cup Lean beef diced
¼ cup chicken livers clean and diced
Black pepper (Optional)
Salt (Optional)
One medium onion diced
Three cloves garlic minced
One teaspoon marjoram
One teaspoon sage
One teaspoon thyme
One cup of potatoes diced ¼ inch cubes
¼ cup flour
Two cups Joanna Marie mixture (recipe page 77)
¼ cup olive oil

In a heavy saucepan render olive oil rabbit, beef, livers, flour, spices, garlic and onions, sautéing on high heat for 30 minutes. Sprinkle ¼ cup flour over frying food. Remove and transfer to medium saucepot. Add Joanna Marie mixture and diced potatoes. Simmer for 30 minutes.

COMMUNITY CHILI

Three pounds ground beef chili meat
Two medium onions minced
Three cloves garlic minced
¼ cup flour
¼ cup olive
¼ cup butter
¼ cup chili powder
One teaspoon thyme
One teaspoon oregano
Three tablespoon brown sugar
One teaspoon cayenne pepper
Salt… (Optional)

In a medium pot add ground chili meat, butter, oil, onions, garlic, sugar, cayenne, spices. Stir well. When bubbly add flour and mix well. Add beef broth, reduce heat simmer for 55 minutes remove. Serve over rice!

BEAN SOUP

One pound navy beans, rinsed and cleaned
Sixty-four ounces vegetable stock
One medium onion diced
½ teaspoon baking soda
Three garlic cloves, crushed
¼ cup olive oil
¼ cup brown sugar
¼ teaspoon butter
One tablespoon fresh basil

In a large cast iron or Dutch oven pot, add all the ingredients. Bring to a boil for 10 minutes and reduce heat. Simmer for 4 hours. Remove from the heat and let cool. Add cooled soup to a blender and puree.

BEEF BROTH

Three pounds beef neck bones
One pound beef shank
¼ cup olive oil
Thirty-two ounces vegetable stock
One cup carrot (tops included)
One tablespoon Bemjag seasoning (recipe page 76)
One cup tomato
Two cups Joanna Marie mix (recipe page 77)
One medium onion
Four garlic cloves, minced

Brown the shank in the oil. Add neck bones, vegetables and stock. Simmer for 2 hours.

GENERATIONAL CHILI

Three pounds ground beef or chili meat
Two medium onions, minced
Three garlic cloves, chopped
½ cup flour
¼ cup olive oil
¼ cup butter
¼ cup chili powder
One teaspoon thyme
One teaspoon oregano
Two tablespoon brown sugar
Two quarts beef stock
One teaspoon Bemjag seasoning (recipe page 76)
Salt to taste

Heat oil and butter to a large pot. Add ground meat, garlic, onions, and spices. Stir well until meat is no longer pink. Add flour into the meat mixture until mixed well and flour is cooked. Stir in the stock and bring to a boil. Simmer for 55-60 minutes. Serve over rice or cornbread.

GALVESTON CLAM CHOWDER

Three pounds fresh clams boiled for 5 minutes (save liquid)
Two quarts fish stock
One cup corned beef diced
¼ pounds potatoes small diced
One large onion minced
Four small ribs of celery minced
¼ cup olive oil
Two tablespoon butter
½ cup flour
½ cup milk
¼ cup clam juice
½ cup heavy cream
Salt and pepper (Optional)
Thyme (Optional)
Worcestershire sauce (Optional)
Hot sauce (Optional)

In a large saucepan add olive oil and butter. Sear the beef. Add onion, garlic, and flour to the pan, stir and mix well. In another cast iron pot heat fish stock to a boil. Add all ingredients except the clams. Simmer for 20 minutes remove from heat, add clams.

SHAKIR'S FULL FLAVORED RED BEANS & RICE

1 pounds red beans (presoaked)
One 2-ounce chicken breast diced
½ gallon chicken stock
One medium onion finely chopped
4 cloves garlic finely minced
¼ cup packed brown sugar
South Texas seasoned rice (recipe page 86)

Add all ingredients to a medium saucepot. Cook for 3 ½ hours. Sear beans on bottom of pot. Stir and keep stirring making certain not to burn. Reduce heat and add chicken breast. Simmer for 20 minutes. Serve with the seasoned rice.

DIGGED DOWN SEAFOOD STEW

Three cups cherry stone clams, cleaned
Four cups cockles' clams, cleaned
Four cups of Atlantic oysters in juice
Three cups tiger shrimp, shells on, deveined
Four cups of firm white fish, Haddock, Atlantic cod, or Pollock
Four cups of blue crab meat
¼ cup strong brewed coffee
One fennel bulb and leaves diced
Three cups onion, diced
One cup red bell pepper, minced
¼ cup minced garlic
Two tablespoons Bemjag seasoning (recipe page 76)
Five cups tomato sauce
Two teaspoon annattos
One quart fish stock
Two cups olive oil
Two cups red grape juice
Salt and pepper to taste

In a large stock pot heat olive oil. Sauté onions, fennel, garlic, spices and pepper. Add the tomato sauce, fish stock and juice. Bring to a boil then simmer for 50 minutes. Add the seafood and simmer for an additional 5 minutes. Remove from heat and serve.

FRUITS & VEGETABLES

MIXED VEGETABLES

1 cup miniature corn
1 cup parsnips
¾ cup snow peas
¾ cup carrots
1 baking white potatoes diced
1 sweet potato diced
1 small rutabaga diced
1 cup leeks, bulb and leaves
¼ cup finely diced onion
1 clove of garlic peel and crushed
1 cup olive oil
½ cup vegetable stock
Salt and white pepper to taste

Cut all vegetables equal in size to ensure even cooking. Blend onion, garlic, vegetable stock, salt, and pepper if desired. Sauté all vegetables in oil except leaves from leeks, until soft but still have a bit of crunchy texture. In a separate saucepan with oil sauté leaves of leeks until tender. Add to sautéed vegetables to and mix well.

BLACK EYE PEAS W/ SMOKED TURKEY NECKS

Two cups presoaked black eye peas
Three quarts chicken stock
½ cup chopped onions
¼ cup chopped garlic
½ cup olive oil
Eight large turkey necks
Salt and white pepper to taste

In a large pot bring stock to a boil. Reduce heat and add remaining ingredients. Bring to a boil and then simmer on low for 80 mins or until beans are tender.

TEJAS MASHED POTATOES

Six medium russet potatoes
One cup milk (hot)
Three tablespoons butter or margarine
One teaspoon brown sugar
One teaspoon cardamom
One teaspoon ginger
Salt and white pepper to taste

Wash, peel and diced the potatoes. Render the potatoes to boiling salted water and cook for 25 minutes. Remove, drain, and cool the potatoes. Make sure the potatoes are dry. Transfer them to a mixing bowl and whip with a handheld mixer for 40 to 50 seconds until the potatoes are smooth and free from lumps. Once completely smooth add the hot milk, butter, and spices. With a rubber spatula scrape the sides of the bowl and continue whipping until the potatoes are smooth and void of lumps. Serve at once.

GRILLED WHITE POTATOES

Two cups sliced white potatoes
One medium onion sliced 2 ½ dia.
Three garlic cloves
Three tablespoons sunflower olive oil
Three teaspoons butter

Place the olive oil and butter on a grill. The grates must be hot before adding the sliced boiled potatoes so they can develop a crust and not absorb much fat. Toss the potatoes while browning them evenly on all sides. Potatoes should be very crispy on the outside and have a soft interior. Sauté onion and garlic. Mix with the potatoes. Serve at once.

LEEKS & CABBAGE MIX

2 cups leeks and lower leaf portion
1 medium cabbage (rolls leaves and cut uniformly)
1 red bell pepper (ribs trimmed and seeded)
2 medium size carrots, toothpick size)
One cup Joanna-Marie mix (recipe page 77)
¼ cup olive oil
1 cup vegetable stock
1 teaspoon cinnamon
1 teaspoon allspice
Salt and white pepper (Optional)

Wash and trim bottom of leeks and core of cabbage and ends of carrots. Set aside for vegetable stock. Render vegetables to medium saucepot. Add oil, vegetable stock, cabbage, leeks, carrots, spices. Cook at high heat for 10 minutes. Reduce heat simmer for 30 minutes. Remove and serve hot over rice.

SAUTEED FENNEL BULBS

Two fennel bulbs, sliced and diced diagonally, fennel ribs diced
One yellow bell pepper
One cup Joanna Marie mix (recipe page 77)
¼ cup olive oil
One medium onion diced
Three garlic cloves minced
One tablespoon brown sugar
¼ teaspoon cinnamon
¼ teaspoon white pepper
Salt to taste

Wash and trim the woody bottom of the fennel bulbs and cut in uniform pieces to ensure even cooking. Cut the top off the bell pepper. Trim the ribs and remove the seeds. In a saucepan, add the oil vegetables and spices. Sauté them until done. Save the leaves as an herb and the seeds of the fennel as a spice.

The delightful licorice or anise flavor of the fennel can be extracted by Grilling, baking, sautéing or steamed. The fennel becomes milder when cooked, it can also be eaten raw. Its peak season for harvesting is September through May. This herb has been a favorite of the Mediterranean people for thousands of years as a vegetable (the bulbs) as an herb (the leaves) as a spice (the seeds.) there are many uses for the fennel; the oral dispensation of the fennel is widely used as remedies in folk and conventional medicine. Water that is extracted from the fennel is used in British pharmacology as a remedy for the excretion of gas and is a tasty sweet palatable additive to many other medicines. From my very own personal experience fennel has been used with other herbs such as thyme, licorice root; and found to reduce mucus in the throat.

STIR FRIED ASPARAGUS

Two cups asparagus
One cup mushroom
One tablespoon canola oil
One clove garlic chopped
Two shallots minced

Wash the asparagus thoroughly. Cut the ends, and slice into two or three pieces. Heat the oil in a saucepan, add the garlic. Begin stirring and frying for 30 seconds. Add the asparagus and simmer until tender.

BAKED BUTTERNUT SQUASH

Three pounds butternut squash thinly sliced
Four tablespoons light butter
One teaspoon allspice
One teaspoon cinnamon
One teaspoon cardamom
Six tablespoon brown sugar
Dash nutmeg
Three tablespoons apple cider

Render the butternut squash seasoned with cardamom, nutmeg, cinnamon, allspice to a casserole dish. Drizzle the cider over the squash. Bake without a cover in a 350° F oven until tender about 40 minutes.

ROASTED CHAYOTE HONEY BUNCH

Four chayote seeded and diced
Two cups butternut squash diced
One cup pear diced (Bosc type)
Three tablespoons butter
One teaspoon cinnamon
1¼ cup honey
Dash nutmeg
Salt (Optional)
One tablespoon brown sugar

Wash and seed the fruit and vegetables. Cut uniformly, to ensure even cooking. Season with the cinnamon and nutmeg. Add the honey, brown sugar and butter to the fruit and vegetables. Place in a baking dish and bake at 350 ° F oven for 45 minutes or until tender.

WHITE POTATOES CRISP

Five pounds russet potatoes
Two cup flour
Two eggs
¼ cup baking powder
2 ½ cups vegetable stock
½ gallon vegetable oil

Wash and cut potatoes one-eighth inch-thick. Prepare batter by mixing flour, salt, eggs, baking powder and three cups vegetable stock in standard mixing bowl. Stir and whip vigorously. Dip fries in batter and render to hot oil at 350 ° F. Cook until brownish.

VEGAN TURNIP GREENS

Two bunches of turnip greens, cleaned and trimmed
One medium onion
¼ cup of honey
¼ teaspoon white pepper
¼ cup grapeseed oil

Place greens, onion, honey, pepper, oil in medium sauce pot. Cook for 2 hours until tender.

TURNIPS SAUTEED & SIMMERED

Peeled and cleaned eight turnips, cubed one-eighth inch-thick
One onion
Two tablespoon butter
One teaspoon olive oil
Two cloves garlic

Place turnips, onions in saucepan with butter and oil simmer for 25 minutes until tender.

MUSTARD COLLARDS & TURNIP GREEN MIX

One bunch mustard- collars- turnips- ea.
One large onion diced
½ cup vegetable oil
Two pounds lamb sausage cooked and sliced
One tablespoon brown sugar
One teaspoon black pepper
Salt (Optional)

Wash greens and stems thoroughly. Set aside stems for vegetable stock. In a large pot cook greens with spices until tender, approximately 3 hours. Render cooked sausage in pot with greens and simmer for 20 minutes.

BLACKEYE PEAS WITH TURKEY HAM

One pound blackeye peas (presoaked)
Two quarts chicken stock
One medium onion diced
Three cloves garlic crushed
¼ cup olive oil
One cup diced turkey ham (cooked)
Salt and white pepper (Optional)

In a sauce pot boil chicken stock, add peas and all ingredients. Cook on high heat for 2 hours. Reduce heat to a simmer. Cook for 45 minutes.

SWEET POTATOES AND MANGO HONEY BUNCH

Three pounds of peeled sliced potatoes
Four medium sized sliced ripe mangos
One cup of honey
½ cup brown sugar packed
½ cup of butter
Two teaspoon allspice
Two teaspoon cinnamon
½ teaspoon nutmeg
Two eggs well beaten

Sauté mangos in a saucepan until caramelized. Pan fry sweet potatoes in butter, cook until slightly tender. Combine sweet potatoes, mango and spices into a baking dish. Cook in a preheated oven at 375 ° F for 30 minutes.

SEARED BAKED RUTABAGA

2 ½ pounds rutabaga cut in cubes
¼ cup of caraway seeds
1/8 cup of dill
¼ grapeseed oil

Place rutabaga in heated oiled saucepan. Sear on all sides. Roll rutabaga cubes in dill and caraway seeds. Add to baking dish. set oven to 300 ° F cook until tender.

CANDIED PINEAPPLE AND MANGO

One whole pineapple
Three medium mangos
One cup brown sugar
One tablespoon honey
One tablespoon agave syrup
One tablespoon granulated sugar (optional)
Three tablespoon butter
¼ teaspoon cinnamon
¼ teaspoon allspice
Pinch of nutmeg
One lemon (juiced)

In saucepan place all ingredients except lemon juice into hot skillet. Cook until sugars are bubbling hot. Reduce heat and simmer for 20 minutes. Place fruit mixture into a casserole dish and drizzle with lemon juice. Bake at 325 ° F until done.

STUFFED BELL PEPPERS

½ cup of assorted vegetables: green beans miniature corn, carrots, parsnips, snow peas, spinach, cabbage, potatoes
¼ cup olive oil
Four green bell peppers
One teaspoon brown sugar
One quart chicken stock
Salt and pepper to taste

Add vegetables to saucepot and cook for 45 minutes. Cut tops of peppers and stuff with vegetables. Place in oven at 300 - 400 ° F until tops are brownish

VEGAN WHITE BEANS

One pound small white beans (presoaked)
½ gallon water or (vegetable stock)
One medium onion
One tablespoon garlic powder
Four ounces tomato paste
One tablespoon basil
¼ cup brown sugar
¼ cup olive oil

Add all ingredients into a medium pot. cook on high heat for 3 ½ hours.
Add salt and pepper to taste.

BEET MERRY BERRY SMOOTHIE

Six garden beets, juiced
Two cups of blackberries, pureed
½ cup honey
½ cup brown sugar
One quart water
Two cups ice

Add juiced beets and remaining ingredients to a blender. Blend until
smooth.

LITE DRIED FRUIT MIX

One ounce pitted dates
One ounce raisins
Four ounce pineapple
Two ounces mango
One ounce peaches
One ounce banana
One ounce apple
One ounce blueberry
¼ cup lite butter
One teaspoon coconut extract
½ cup honey

In saucepan heat butter. Add all fruit except blueberries. Stir and cook for 10 minutes. Add the coconut extract and honey. Stir and simmer for an additional five minutes. Top off with blueberries. Excellent on pancakes and waffles.

SEARED GREEN BEANS WITH WHITE POTATOES

Two pounds green beans
Three white potatoes sliced and cooked
¼ cup olive oil
Two tablespoon garlic crushed
Four shallots finely chopped
One cup vegetable stock
One teaspoon white pepper
One teaspoon cumin
Salt... (Optional)

Wash, peel and slice potatoes. In a medium pot, add to boiling water cook for 20 minutes or until done. Wash and clean beans. Place in boiling water for 8 minutes remove from heat. Submerge beans in cold water halting the cooking process. Combine beans, potatoes, and vegetable stock. simmer in saucepan 10 minutes.

CANDIED HONEY YAMS

Three pounds yams
One cup butter
One teaspoon cinnamon
One teaspoon allspice
Dash nutmeg
½ cup brown sugar
One cup honey
Salt (Optional)

Brown yams on all sides in a buttery hot saucepan. Add ingredients and simmer for 20 minutes.

BROCCOLI "N" CREAM CHEESE PECAN SAUCE

Two crowns of broccoli
Two tablespoon crushed pecans
Eight broccoli spears cut in small pieces
Four ounces cream cheese
Two tablespoon milk
Two tablespoon of olive oil
Three teaspoon of honey
One clove of garlic
One small red onion sliced

Wash broccoli under cold water. Heat oil in saucepan. Add broccoli and cook until semi crunchy. Place onion, garlic, broccoli spears, cream cheese and honey in saucepan. Sauté until golden brown. Place the mixture into a blender. Blend until smooth and pour over cooked broccoli. Add Salt and pepper if desired.

PAN FRIED OKRA TOMATOES

Two small tomatoes
One pound okra
One teaspoon brown sugar
One medium onion
Dash cayenne
¼ cup vegetable oil

Wash and cut ends of okra and tops of tomatoes. In a medium saucepan with oil, render okra. Reduce heat and simmer for 30 minutes. Add tomatoes and keep simmering for 10 minutes.

STIR FRIED BOK CHOY

Three pounds bok choy, pick leaves apart and slice ribs diagonally
One medium onion
One red bell pepper seeded ribs trimmed, cut into toothpick sizes
¼ cup olive oil
¼ teaspoon brown sugar
Salt and pepper (Optional)

Add oil to saucepan. Sauté bok choy, bell pepper and onion. Add in the brown sugar. Stir fry for 15 minutes.

GENERATIONAL MASHED POTATOES

Five cups diced medium sized potato
One cup milk
Three tablespoon olive oil
One teaspoon brown sugar
One teaspoon ginger
Salt and white pepper to taste

Boil potatoes until fork tender. Drain well and add to a mixing bowl. Mix potatoes until smooth. Heat milk, butter and spices, stirring until sugar dissolves. Add the milk mixture to the potatoes until mixed well.

GRILLED SPICY POTATOES

Six cups sliced potatoes (any variety)
½ cup annatto spice mix
½ cup olive oil
½ cup butter

Prepare the grill by scraping charred debris from grill. Mix the spice, olive oil and butter together. Place the potatoes on the grilled. Brush the potatoes with the mixture. Flip and turn the potatoes until crusty on the outside, soft inside.

COKE BATTERED ONION RINGS

One cup of flour
Three teaspoon baking powder
Salt to taste
White pepper to taste
One egg beaten
12 ounce Coke soda
Three pounds whole onions slice rings
Flour as needed for dredging

Preheat oil in a large pot or dutch oven to 350 °. Mix the dry ingredients well, add the coke and egg making a smooth batter. Add onions rings to the flour then to the batter. Dip the rings in hot oil.

BAKED POTATOES STUFFED WITH BACON

Six russet potatoes
Two cups hot milk three tablespoons butter
½ cup turkey bacon or your choice of bacon
Three scallions minced
Paprika (Optional)
Salt and pepper (Optional)
Nutmeg (Optional)
Allspice (Optional)
Parmesan cheese finely grated

Scrub the potatoes and pierce the skin of each potato with a fork. This allows the steam to escape. Rub the potatoes with oil. Bake in a 475 ° F oven for an hour or until done. Cut in half and carefully scoop out the flesh leaving the shells intact. Mix the potatoes with the above ingredients except the cheese. spoon the potato mixture back into the shells. top with cheese sprinkle with paprika, salt and pepper if desired.

FRIED CRISPY ZUCCHINI SQUASH

½ dozen zucchini squash
½ cup of flour
½ cup course meal
½ cup baking powder
One cup of milk
One cup of olive oil
Two eggs, cracked and beaten well

Slice squash into ¼ inch thick rounds. Place dry ingredients into a shallow dish and eggs into a separate shallow dish. Dredge squash in eggs and then into the flour mixture. Place into hot skillet and fry until golden brown.

BAKED LEEKS-N-VEGETABLE DISH

Four ribs of leeks wash and diced
One small celery root washed and diced
½-cup butternut squash wash and diced
One cup carrot wash and diced
¼ cup lemon juice
¼-cup butter
One tablespoon brown sugar
One tablespoon cardamom
Salt and pepper (Optional)

Wash the vegetables peel and cut them as instructed above. Carefully cut all vegetables into uniform shapes and sizes. Rub them with spices and oil before rendering them to baking dish. To promote even cooking and an attractive finish product, vegetables should be baked separately then combined at the time when served. Light colored vegetable retains color with acid such as lemon juice. After baking them separately, combine them and render them to a serving dish.

CASSEROLES & SALADS

NOPALES RICE CASSEROLE

Two cactuses pads, nopales
One cup Joanna-Marie mix (recipe page 77)
One pound long grain rice, cooked
One medium onion
One tablespoon black cumin
One red bell pepper diced
¼ cup olive oil
¼ cup vegetable stock

Wash, cut and trim the cactus pads using tongs. With a sharp knife cut off the thorns and eyes of the nopales. Add olive oil, onions, peppers and nopales to a saucepan. Cook the onions until they are translucent. Render the vegetables and cooked rice to a baking dish. Bake at 350 ° F for twenty minutes. Remove from oven sprinkle cumin over rice liberally.

BESSIE MAE MAC & CHEESE

Two cups uncooked macaroni
½ cup minced onion
One tablespoon minced garlic
¼ cup vegetable base
¼ cup Bemjag seasoning (recipe page 76)
¼ cup butter
Three eggs beaten
¼ cup olive oil
Two quarts of water
One cup vegetable stock

Bring to boil two quarts of water. Add macaroni and boil for five minutes. Remove from heat and cover with the lid. Let stand for 20 minutes. Strain the macaroni and add to a casserole dish. set aside. In the meantime, add the vegetable base, olive oil, butter seasoning, stock, eggs, onion and garlic to a blender. Blend well and pour into the casserole dish. Fold in one cup of cheddar cheese. Sprinkle remaining cheese on top. Place in a preheated 355 °F oven. Bake for 25 minutes on top rack.

POTATOES W/ SHALLOTS CASSEROLE

Three white potatoes slice very thin
½ cup of thinly cut shallots
Sixteen ounces of mild cheddar cheese, shredded
1/8 cup of grapeseed oil
¼ teaspoon white pepper
One tablespoon honey

Peel and wash potatoes. Place oil, potatoes, onions, and honey in a
saucepan. Sauté until golden brown. Add to a casserole dish and sprinkle
with shredded cheese. Cook in oven at 325 ° F for 15 minutes.

BEAN VEGETABLE SALAD

One cup each canned, strained red, white & black beans
Two heads of chopped lettuce
¼ cup sliced carrots
¼ cup chopped celery
¼ cup sliced beets
¼ cup lemon juice
One cup plain yogurt
¼ cup Dock It Sauce (recipe page 76)

Add above ingredients to a salad bowl and chill in the refrigerator for at
least 2 hours.

CUCUMBER ONION CARROT SALAD

One medium onion sliced
Two cucumbers sliced
½ cup vinegar
One cup of carrots sliced
¼ cup olive oil
¼ cup dill

In a bowl, mix cucumber, carrots and onion with vinegar. Toss well.
Add salt and pepper (optional)

ROASTED CHESTNUT VEGETABLE CASSEROLE

Three pounds water chestnuts peeled and diced
One large butter nut squash mashed
Eight ounce bamboo shoots diced
One pound yams sliced
One cup of fennel... diced the bulbs
One tablespoon allspice
¼ cup olive oil

Add the chestnuts to saucepan, cook until golden brown. Place the fennel,
squash and yams in casserole. Spread the chestnuts on top. Bake and roast
at 375 ° F for 35 minutes

CORNBREAD DRESSING

Prepared cornbread (recipe page 99)
Two teaspoon thyme
Two tablespoon sage
One teaspoon marjoram
One teaspoon rosemary
One teaspoon nutmeg
One teaspoon black pepper
One cup chicken stock

Crumble cornbread into a large mixing bowl. Add seasonings and stock, mix well. Bake @ 350 ° F for 20 minutes or until golden brown

SPINACH POTATO KALE CASSEROLE

Three sliced potatoes
One cup of finely chopped kale
Sixteen ounce mozzarella cheese
One pound of chopped spinach
One egg well beaten
¼ cup half milk half cream
¼ cup of olive oil
One tablespoon butter
½ cup vegetable stock

Cook spinach and kale for 20 minutes. Add salt, and pepper… (optional). In a mixing bowl, fold in eggs and cheese, stir in the milk and cream. In another saucepan brown potatoes. Add the greens and the cream mixture to a casserole dish. Cook at 350 ° F in oven for 30 minutes.

JUST SALAD & LEMON SAUCE

One head romaine lettuce
Three tomatoes
Three parsnips diced
Two curve neck squash cut thin
One red apple diced
One tablespoon olive oil
¼ lemon juice
One tablespoon arrowroot
¼ cup olive oil

In a small bowl mix the lemon juice and oil. In a separate mixing bowl add the vegetables and mix with the sauce. Toss well and serve.

AUNT MAUZIA POTATO SALAD

Six cups diced potatoes, cooked
¼ cup minced onions
Two garlic cloves
One tablespoon bemjag seasonings (recipe page 76)
¾ cup mayonnaise
¼ cup mustard
¼ cup pimentos
Two tablespoons olive oil
2 ½ cups boiled eggs, chopped

Sauté onion and garlic until translucent and fragrant. In a mixing bowl, add the remaining ingredients and potatoes. Mix well and chill in the refrigerator before serving.

PARSNIP POTATO CARROT DISH

Three pounds parsnips sliced
Two pounds carrots sliced
Two pounds russet potatoes sliced
¼ cup Heavy cream
Five ounces unsalted butter

Cut all vegetables in equal portions to ensure even cooking. Boil the vegetables separately in a medium sauce pot. Drain the vegetables well and combine them into a baking dish. Add the butter and cream over the vegetables. Bake at 350 ° F for 20 minutes.

SWEET POTATO PUDDING

Six large, sweet potatoes
One cup butter
½ cup flour
Two cups brown sugar
½ cup milk
One tablespoon cinnamon
Four eggs beaten
¼ teaspoon nutmeg
¼ teaspoon ginger

In a mixing bowl whip, the potatoes until smooth. Add the remaining ingredients. Stir well and add to baking dish. Bake at 350 ° F for 35 minutes.

POTATOES LAYERED WITH CHEESE

Two pounds russet potatoes sliced
Two cups Cheddar cheese
Three tablespoon butter or as needed
Four egg yolks
One cup half and half
Salt and pepper to taste

In a well-greased baking pan of layer, the potatoes and cheese making the top layer cheese. Blend the egg, butter, and cream together. Pour the mixture on top. Bake at 250 ° F for 60 minutes or until brownish.

GOODY GOOD RICE PUDDING

Sixteen ounces long grain rice
Two eggs beaten
Two teaspoons vanilla extract
Four teaspoons lemon juice
Three cups water
¼ cup butter
½ cup milk
½ cup brown sugar
¼ cup granulated sugar

In a medium pot bring to boil 1 quart of water just covering the rice. cook for 20 minutes. Remove from stove top. In mixing bowl render rice, sugar, and spices, fold in beaten eggs. Bake at 350 ° F for 20 minutes until brownish.

BREAD PUDDING

Fifteen slices stale bread, diced
¼ cup peaches
¼ cup grapes
Four eggs
¼ cup pineapples
¼ cup cherries
One cup pineapple juice
One cup granulated sugar
¼ cup brown sugar
One tablespoon vanilla
Two teaspoon lemon extract
One cup butter

In a medium stock pot render all fruit, sugar, butter, extracts and juice.
Bring to a simmer for 30 minutes. Remove from heat. Add bread toa
casserole dish and cover with the cooked fruit mixture. Slide into an oven
at 325° F for 20 minutes.

HAIL SPAGHETTI

Sixteen ounces uncooked spaghetti
Two cups of vegetable stock
Two cups of chicken stock
Two cups of beef stock
One teaspoon annatto
Three cups of shredded cheddar cheese
½ cup plain yogurt
½ cup sour cream
Two spice bags

Par boil spaghetti and strain. Add to a large stock pot with the stocks,
annatto, spice bags, yogurt and sour cream. Simmer for 20 minutes. Strain
and cool. Place in a casserole dish and top with cheese. Bake in a preheated
300 °F oven for 30 minutes.

SOUTH TEXAS SEASONED RICE

Two cups long grain rice
One quart chicken stock
¼ cup bell peppers diced
½ cup onions crushed and minced
Three cloves garlic crushed and minced
¼ cup pimentos diced
One tablespoon cumin
One tablespoon brown sugar
One tablespoon turmeric
½ cup olive oil
Salt and white pepper (Optional)

In a medium sauce pot add rice, onion, garlic, chicken stock, peppers, and oil. Bring to a rolling boil. Reduce heat to low temperature and simmer for 30 minutes until rice is flaky. Add more chicken stock if necessary and continue to cook. Once done add pimentos and if desired, salt and pepper place in a baking display dish and sprinkle cumin liberally over rice.

SWEET & SAVORY CAKES, BREADS

CAST IRON BAKED CORNBREAD

Two cups of corn meal
¼ cup flour
Two tablespoon baking powder
Two tablespoon salt
¼ cup brown sugar
One cup of milk
One cup butter milk
Three eggs
¾ cup olive oil

Preheat oven to 350 °F. Place a greased cast iron skillet to heat up while preparing the batter. Sift all dry ingredients into mixing bowl. Add milk, eggs and oil. Mix well. Add batter to hot cast iron skillet. Bake for 40 minutes. Remove and cool.

HOT WATER CORNBREAD

Two cups cornmeal
two tablespoons brown sugar
¼ cup olive oil
I cup boiling hot water

Mix cornmeal with sugar and oil with a portion scoop measure and roll mixture into a patty drop into saucepan with hot oil fry on both sides 10 minutes.

CLABBER MILK CORNMEAL PANCAKES

1 cup white or wheat flour
1 cup cornmeal yellow dry from whole grain
1 tablespoon brown or granulated sugar
1 teaspoon baking powder
½ teaspoon soda
Salt (Optional)
Two eggs
Two cups clabber milk or buttermilk
½ cup vegetable oil

In a medium bowl, sift dry ingredients together. In a separate medium bowl add all wet ingredients. Stir and mix well, dry and wet ingredients. Using a two-inch ladle drop pancakes batter on well-greased grill. When browned on one side and bubbles appear, flip the pancake, and cooked until both sides are brown. Repeat the process for more pancakes.

LEMON NUT BREAD

2 ½ cups flour
Three eggs
One cup granulated sugar
One tablespoon baking powder
1 ¼ cup milk
¾ cup grated lemon peel
1 ½ cups walnuts
Thirteen walnut halves
¼ cup butter softened
One teaspoon salt

In a mixing bowl, mix butter and sugar, until creamy. Whip in eggs gradually. Add flour, salt, baking powder and milk. Mix until smooth. Fold in lemon peel and chopped walnuts. Pour into greased floured pan of your choice. Top off with walnut halves. Bake at 350 ° F for 65 minutes. Allow 10 minutes to cool.

AUNT MAUZIA'S GINGERBREAD

Three cups flour sifted
One large egg beaten
Two teaspoon baking soda
One teaspoon ground clove
1 ½ teaspoon cinnamon
1 ½ teaspoon ginger
One teaspoon salt
One cup shortening
One cup granulated sugar
1½ cup molasses
1 ½ cup hot water

In a large bowl, mix shortening with sugar. Add the egg until light and fluffy. Beat in molasses at a low speed beat. To the mixture add hot water. Mix until smooth. Pour into standard size baking pan of your choice lined with waxed paper. Bake at 350 ° F for 55-60 minutes till done.

BANANA NUTTY NUT BREAD

2 ¼ cups flour (all purpose or wheat)
Two teaspoons baking powder
¼ teaspoon soda
¾ teaspoon ground cinnamon
Dash ground nutmeg
Pinch ground ginger
1 ¼ cup sugar (granulated)
½ cup confectionary sugar (for topping)
¼ cup cream
Salt to taste
Three medium eggs lightly beaten
¾ cups vegetable oil
1 ¾ cups banana, mashed
¼ cup Pecans, chopped
¼ cup almonds, chopped
¼ cup Walnuts

Preheat oven at 350 ° F and grease the bottom of a baking pan. In a large mixing bowl combine all dry ingredients. In a separate bowl mix all wet ingredients (bananas included) with dry ingredients. Mix until lumpy. Fold in the walnuts. If desired, you can make a topping for the batter. In small bowl mix one tablespoon butter, two tablespoon flour, ¼ cup cream ¼ cup confectionary sugar. Fold in the remaining nuts and spread over the batter. Slide pan in preheated oven and bake for 60 minutes. Remove and sprinkle with confectionary sugar.

BUTTERMILK COFFEE PANCAKES

Twelve ounces of white flour
Four ounces whole wheat
Three tablespoon granulated sugar
Sixteen ounces buttermilk
Eight ounces coffee (brewed)
Three ounce unsalted butter
Five eggs beaten
Clarified butter (Optional)

Combine and sift dry ingredients. Mix the wet ingredients together with the dry ingredients. Grease the griddle with butter and set the temperature to 375 ° F. Using a two ounce ladle, drop portions of batter on the griddle plate. When bubbles appear on the surface and the bottom is brown, flip the pancake and cook on the other side until brown. Repeat the process with the remaining batter.

SWEET POTATO PANCAKES

Two cups wheat or all-purpose flour
One tablespoon of baking powder
One tablespoon brown sugar
Salt (Optional)
One teaspoon cinnamon
¼ teaspoon ground nutmeg
¼ teaspoon ground ginger
1 ¾ cups milk
¼ cup sweet potatoes
Two eggs beaten
Two tablespoons vegetable oil

Sift flour, baking powder, sugar, and spices into a large mixing bowl. Add eggs, milk, and the sweet potatoes. Stir vigorously for two minutes until smooth. Dip batter out with a two-inch ladle spread batter on a greased or skillet. Cook until bubbles appear when pancakes are brown flip and brown on the other side. Repeat the process. Homemade syrup recipe shown on page 79.

WHEAT PANCAKES WITH SUNFLOWER SEEDS

One cup whole wheat flour
¾ cup all-purpose flour
One tablespoon brown sugar
Two teaspoon baking powder
Pinch of baking soda
Salt (Optional)
One large egg beaten
1 ¾ cups buttermilk
¼ cup bottled spring water
Three tablespoon vegetable oil
Handful shelled sunflower seeds

In a large bowl stir together all dry ingredients. In a separate bowl combine eggs, milk and oil with a wire whisk. Add the liquid ingredients to the dry ingredients and mix well. The batter should be moist and lumpy. Preheat a skillet or griddle. Using a two-inch portion ladle; scoop the batter onto a griddle or into a hot cast iron skillet. Remove and serve, spread the unsalted sunflower seeds liberally over the syrup and pancakes.

DIPS, SAUCES & SEASONING MIXES

COLD SMOKED SEASONING

Six ounces cumin
Four ounces chili powder
Six ounces paprika
Six ounces cardamom
Three ounces nutmeg
Three ounces allspice
Sixteen ounce cayenne
One ounce salt

Place all ingredients in wooden bowl (made from oak)
Place bowl in smoker.
Choice of wood: pecan, oak, mesquite. Smoke spices at 50° F – 85 °F for eight hours.

BEMJAG SEASONING

One tablespoon dried garlic
One tablespoon dried onion
½ cup brown sugar
One tablespoon cumin
One teaspoon nutmeg
One teaspoon red pepper flakes
One teaspoon allspice
One teaspoon oregano
One teaspoon thyme
One teaspoon sage
½ tablespoon salt

Mix above ingredients well. Store in airtight containers.

JOANNA-MARIE MIX

Four medium onions (diced)
One pound of carrots
Two stalks of celery
Two bell peppers (remove ribs)

Cut and dice vegetables store in freezer bags for future use.

AVOCADO JALAPENO DIP

Five very ripe small avocados
Two cloves garlic
One shallot
One tablespoon butter
Two jalapeno peppers sliced and diced
One teaspoon brown sugar
One tablespoon apple cider vinegar
¼ cup shallots, pureed
Salt (Optional)

In a mixing bowl place avocado and vigorously whip. In a blender, blend garlic, shallot, sugar, and vinegar until smooth. Add blended ingredients to avocados. Fold peppers into mixture. Chill until ready to serve.

MEAN BEAN CHEDDAR DIP

Two cups pinto beans
Two shallots
Two cloves garlic
½ cup shredded cheddar
One tablespoon apple cider vinegar
Salt (Optional)

In a mixing bowl, stir beans until smooth. In a saucepan, sauté with oil and butter, the shallots and garlic. Remove from heat and add them in a blender. Add the blended ingredients with the mashed beans. Stir together well. When ready to serve, top off with cheddar.

DOCK IT SAUCE

¼ cup fennel bulb, chopped
One beet diced
One cup tomato sauce
One quart seafood stock
One teaspoon sage
One teaspoon marjoram
One teaspoon thyme
Two teaspoon brown sugar
Two teaspoon onion powder
Two teaspoon garlic powder
¼ cup cornstarch

Place above ingredients in a blender and use the liquefy setting. Once done pour in a heated oiled skillet and bring to a boil. Reduce heat and simmer for 20 minutes. Let cool and place in an airtight squirt bottle.

HOME MADE MAPLE SYRUP

Three cups brown sugar
One cup white sugar
One teaspoon rosemary extract (preservative)
One tablespoon maple extract
Three cups of water
½ tablespoon butter

In a cast iron skillet, add the white sugar and caramelize it. Then add brown sugar, extracts, butter, and water. Simmer for 30 minutes.

SEAFOOD

FISH SANDWICH

Six fish fillets (whiting or trout)
Six slices of cheddar cheese
½ cup olive oil
One cup of flour
One white potato, thin sliced
Mayonnaise or mustard
Sliced onions
One teaspoon salt
One cup pickle juice
One teaspoon dillweed

In a shallow dish sprinkle the fish with flour and salt making sure to cover on both sides. Pan fry in a heated skillet cooking until done. In separate saucepan on high heat brown the potatoes. Reduce heat and cook until done. In a blender put one cup of pickle juice and dill. Blend until liquidly. Add to a squeeze bottle. On two slices of your choice of bread, add the sliced onions, potatoes, your choice of Mayo or mustard and cheese. Add the fish and drizzle with the pickle juice blend over the fish.

SKILLET FRIED CATFISH

Four large catfish cut in half
One cup vegetable oil
Six ounces of flour
Ten ounces corn meal
One pint of buttermilk
One teaspoon ginger
One teaspoon chili powder
Two tablespoon white pepper
Two tablespoon salt

Combine all dry ingredients. Dredge fish in buttermilk. Preheat a cast iron skillet and add the vegetable oil. Dredge fish in prepared flour and spice mix, render fish to skillet. Sear heavily on each side, cook 5 minutes.

WHOLLY SMOKE MACKEREL

Forty-eight pacific or Atlantic mackerel
Cold smoked seasoning (recipe page 76)

Roll fish in a liberal amount of cold smoked seasoning. Place mackerel in
smoke box. Smoke at 250 ° F for 3 hours

JUST RED SNAPPER

2 ½ pounds red snapper
Three tablespoons butter
One teaspoon dill
One tablespoon lemon juice
Salt and pepper

Score the skin of the fillet with diagonal 1/8 inch deep cuts. Season the
fillet with salt and pepper. Brush with melted butter and sprinkle with dill.
Place the fillet in broiler skin side up. Remove from broiler. Serve the fish
on a bed of radish leaves and drizzle with lemon juice liberally on top of
fish.

SOUTH TEXAS FLOUNDER

Three flounders fillet medium size
Two tablespoons light butter
One medium onion
Two cloves garlic
¼ cup olive oil
¼ cup flour
One cup fish stock
Two teaspoon dill weed
¼ cup heavy cream
Two teaspoon cinnamon

Render ½ butter and ½ olive oil to sheet pan, arrange flounder onto the pan. bake at 400 ° F for 15 minutes. Remove from oven and set aside. In a saucepan, add the remaining butter, oil, flour, onions, garlic and spices. stir well. Making a roux add the fish stock and heavy cream. Stir until the desired thickness. Pour creamed gravy on the flounder.

STEWED- SOFT SHELL CRABS

Three pounds soft shell crab wash and clean
Two cups white potatoes diced small
One medium onion
Four cloves garlic
One teaspoon sage
 One teaspoon marjoram
One teaspoon thyme
One teaspoon allspice
Two quarts chicken stock
½ cup olive oil
¼ cup flour

In a saucepan add oil, onions, garlic and potatoes over high heat. Stir until onions are translucent. Add small amounts of flour stirring for about 10 minutes. Transfer all ingredients to a medium pot with two quarts chicken stock. Bring to a rolling boil and add the potatoes. cook 10 minutes. After stock resume boiling, remove from heat and add soft shell crab. Cover with a tight-fitting lid. Return saucepot to heat. Let stand for 20 minutes. Serve.

DEEP FRIED WHITING FILLET FISH

Ten pieces fillet fish
One cup flour
One tablespoon baking powder
One cup fish stock
One quart of vegetable oil
One cup buttermilk
¼ cup dill
Salt and black pepper (Optional)
Four shallots minced
Five cloves garlic minced

In a blender mix buttermilk, fish stock, garlic, onions, salt and black pepper until smooth. In another mixing dish render flour, dill and baking powder. Place blended batter in a separate dish. Pat and flip fillet fish in flour mixture. Remove fillet fish and add to blended batter. In a medium fry pot add oil, heat at 350 ° F. Drop four pieces of fillet at a time. Fry for 10 minutes or until fish floats.

CRAB VEGETABLE BOIL

Ten white potatoes quartered
One dozen eggs
Four pounds blue crabs washed clean
Sixteen ounces olive oil
Three pounds carrots sliced one-eighth inch thick
Five sweet potatoes quartered
Two whole ancho peppers
Three whole jalapeno peppers
One tablespoon ground cayenne pepper

In a ten gallon stock, pot add six gallons water boil the eggs for 15 minutes. Remove boiled eggs and add all vegetables, peppers, seasonings and crabs. Boil for 20 more minutes, remove from heat. let set…enjoy

WHITE CRAB CAKES

Eighteen ounces white crab meat
One small red bell pepper minced
One small green bell pepper minced
One bunch scallion sliced
One cup stale breadcrumbs diced
Light butter melted your…discretion
Two small eggs beaten
Worcestershire sauce … (Optional)
Hot sauce … (Optional)
Mustard… (Optional)

Sauté the bell peppers in a pat of butter until tender. Place the cream in a saucepan and bring to a boil. remove from heat and cool. Combine the ingredients listed above except the breadcrumbs into a mixing boil. Mix well. With an ice cream scoop form the cakes in a patty, the scoop will ensure uniformity. Press the breadcrumbs into the cakes. Place the cakes in a skillet with a moderate amount of butter and brown on each side. Remove and drain the crab cakes.

SALMON CROQUETTES

Thirty-two ounces salmon, flaked
One medium onion diced
Two garlic cloves diced
¼ teaspoon brown sugar
½ cup olive oil
One cup flour
One cup cornmeal
¼ teaspoon cream of tartar
1 ½ tablespoon baking powder

Sauté onions and garlic until onions become translucent. Once cooked, mix in a bowl with the remaining ingredients. Form mixture into patties. Cook until outside is browned and crispy, approx. 5 – 6 mins per side.

GRILLED SALMON

Three pounds salmon
¼ cup olive oil
½ cup bemjag seasoning (recipe page 76)

Preheat grill to 375 °F. Brush salmon with olive oil. Season both sides.
Place on skin side down on grill. Grill for 5 – 7 minutes per side.

SEA BASS W/ SAUTEED LEEKS

Four pounds sea bass with skin on
Two ribs of leeks
Four tablespoon butter
¼ teaspoon turmeric
¼ teaspoon cinnamon
¼ teaspoon dill
¼ teaspoon allspice

Render spices and butter into blender, blend well into a smooth mixture.
Score fish with diagonal cuts ¼ inch deep. Brush with butter and spice
mixture. Place fish into broiler and cook until when pierce with a knife, it
flakes. Place leeks in medium saucepot boiling briefly about 15 minutes.
Remove submerge in cold water stopping the cooking process. When
cooled cut the leeks into small toothpick sizes. Render leeks under bass on
plate.

STUFFED BANANA PEPPERS W/ WILD CAUGHT TUNA

Two pounds wild caught tuna
½ cup smoked oysters
¼ cup onions
Two ounces of fish stock
¼ tablespoon olive oil
Salt and pepper... (Optional)

Cook wild caught tuna and onion in lightly oil saucepan for 5 minutes. Add oysters. Cut banana peppers horizontally and stuff batter with ingredients. Bake in oven at 350 ° F for 15 minutes.

SALMON SORREL

Three pounds salmon
One bunch sorrel leaves (chopped)
Twelve parsnips diced cook; boiling
One red pepper diced
One cup eggplant diced
Three shallots diced
One teaspoon brown sugar
One teaspoon dill
¼ cup fish stock
Three tablespoons butter
¼ cup milk
Salt and white pepper to taste

Wash and score the salmon with diagonal cuts 1/8inch deep.
Bake salmon at 350 ° F for twenty minutes do not overcook. Wash all
vegetables cut and peel the parsnips. Trim off the ends of the bell peppers
cut away the seeds and the core, cut away the ribs and slice them. Chop
the leaves of the sorrel. In a medium pot add parsnips to boiling salted
water for twenty minutes. Remove from heat. The parsnips must be dry for
mashing. Add fish stock, eggplant, bell pepper and sorrel to a skillet and
sauté. In a bowl add the parsnips, butter and milk. Stir and whip until they
are smooth and firm. Place the scored salmon on a platter. Pour the
sautéed vegetables with its juices onto the salmon. With a portion scoop,
scoop out the mashed parsnips; add a sorrel leaf for garnish.

SHRIMP W/CRABMEAT OVER CORNBREAD DRESSING

Four cups large shrimp (deveined)
Two tablespoons flour
One cup ¾ ounces white crab meat
One cup ¾ ounces fish stock
One teaspoon cinnamon
One teaspoon turmeric
Three shallots, diced
Three garlic cloves, minced
One tablespoon light butter
¼ cup olive oil
Prepared cornbread dressing (recipe page 60)

In a saucepan heat oil and butter. Reduce heat and add onion, garlic, cinnamon, and turmeric. Sauté until onions are translucent. Add flour, making a roux. Stir and cook for 10 minutes. Add the fish stock. Stir. When slightly thickened add shrimp and crabmeat with juices. Simmer for 5 minutes. Serve over the cornbread.

BRUNCH

AUNT ELLEN HASH BROWNS

Three large shredded white potatoes
¼ cup olive oil

Place olive oil in saucepan set burner at medium heat. Add potatoes turn repeatedly until golden brown. Serve with eggs and homemade sausage of your choice.

ANCHO PEPPERS STUFFED W/ POTATO & EGG

Six eggs well beaten
Two russet potatoes (peeled and diced)
¼ cup olive oil
Six ancho peppers
Salt (Optional)

Place diced potatoes in saucepan, fry until soft. Remove from heat. Place in mixing bowl and mix until smooth and firm. Place eggs in saucepan scramble eggs with remaining olive oil. Add eggs to the potatoes and mix. Slice ancho pepper horizontally and stuff with potatoes and egg.

SOUTHERN SWEET POTATO CREPES

One pound of flour
Eight ounces granulated sugar
Salt (Optional)
Seven whole eggs
Seven egg yolks
Two cups sweet potatoes, cooked and mashed
Twelve ounces water
Eight ounces milk
Eight ounces unsalted butter, melted
Ghee (clarified butter) as needed

Combine sweet potatoes with other ingredients stir in melted butter. Let set for about an hour before cooking. Heat a skillet coated with Ghee butter. Using a two ounce ladle pour the batter into skillet covering the bottom. Cook the crepe until light brown approximately 35 seconds.

GRITS SUM WAY

Twelve medium shrimp deveined
¼ cup butter melted
One cup grits
¼ cup crab meat
One tablespoon flour
Five cups fish stock
Salt and pepper (Optional)

In a medium sauce pot render grits and five cups fish stock. Bring to a boil. Reduce heat and simmer for 25 minutes. In a saucepan add butter, crabmeat and shrimp. Add flour and the remaining stock. Cook and stir for 5 minutes. Scoop ¼ cup crab meat and shrimp place in blender making a creamy sauce. Reheat and serve over grits, shrimp and crab.

BLUEBERRY PANCAKE PUDDING

Ten small fist size pancakes cut and cubed
1 ½ pint fresh blueberries
¾ cup granulated sugar
One tablespoon lemon juice
¼ cup water
Pinch allspice
¼ cup melted butter

In a saucepan heat water, blueberry, sugar, lemon juice, butter, and allspice. Cooked until blueberries are rendered down. Place mixture into a bowl and chill. Add cubed pancakes to the chilled blueberry sauce, mix well. Top off with whipping cream.

BUTTERMILK BISCUITS

Three cups of flour
One cup of buttermilk
One ½ cup of butter
One tablespoon sugar
One teaspoon salt

Preheat oven to 350 ° F. Add flour, one cup butter, sugar, salt and baking powder into a mixing bowl. Mix until pea shaped balls appear. Add milk and knead until moist. Form into medium size balls. Brush with remaining melted butter. Place onto a warm baking pan, let stand for 20 minutes. Bake for 25 minutes or until tops have turned slightly brown.

WATERMELON DRINK

Sixty-four ounces fresh watermelon juice
Two cups cane sugar
Three lemons sliced
Three teaspoons watermelon extract

Mix all ingredients into a large container. Stir well and refrigerate overnight.

WORD UP FRENCH TOAST

Slice bread 1 day ole one inch thick
Three eggs
One cup heavy cream
One teaspoon salt
One teaspoon allspice
One teaspoon nutmeg
One tablespoon cinnamon
¼ cup butter

With a wire whisk, briskly beat eggs, cream, salt, cinnamon, allspice nutmeg together. Dip bread into mix and let soak. Melt butter into cast iron skillet on high heat. Rendering bread slices to hot buttered skillet and brown on both sides.

EGGS-CRAB MEAT-HOMINY

One cup crabmeat
One cup hominy
½ cup butter
Twelve eggs
½ cup milk or heavy cream

In a mixing bowl combine eggs, milk, or heavy cream. Beat vigorously with a wire whisk. Heat butter in a sauté pan. Pour the eggs mixture into the hot pan, stirring frequently until set. Remove eggs from the pan. Add butter, hominy and crab meat. Stir and cook until slightly golden in color. Add in the eggs. Mix well. Remove from heat and serve.

SKILLET FRIED EGGS SOUTHERN STYLE

¼ butter or margarine
Three tablespoon dried breadcrumbs
One cup grated cheddar cheese
Six eggs
Two medium onions sliced very thin
Salt and pepper (Optional)

Render butter in skillet with onions. Sweat the onions until tender. Break eggs over onions. Sprinkle with salt and peppers. Top with crumbs and cheese. Cover with a heavy lid. Cook for 10 minutes and serve.

PUNCH PUNCH-IN

One gallon club soda
Three pounds seedless grapes red or green
Two cinnamon sticks
Two cloves anise
Three cups granulated sugar
Six whole allspice
½ gallon pomegranate juice
½ gallon raspberry juice
¼ teaspoon almond extract
One huge punch bowl
Two pound bag of ice

In a large stockpot combine the pomegranate juice, cinnamon, sugar, and allspice. Bring to a boil and reduce heat. Simmer for five minutes. Strain the mixture through a cheesecloth and china cap. Place grapes on bottom of punch bowl. Add ice, pomegranate mixture, club soda, and almond extract. Serve immediately.

EGG-O-OMELET

One medium onion finely chopped
One bell pepper seeded remove ribs and finely chop
Twelve eggs
½ cup pimentos
½ cup butter
One cup milk
Salt and pepper (Optional)

Sauté the onion and bell pepper in an omelet skillet and remove, set aside.
In a bowl whisk the eggs together. Season with salt and pepper and pour
the eggs into the hot buttered omelet skillet. Reduce heat as the omelet
began to set. Spoon the cooked onions and bell pepper along with the
pimentos onto the omelet. Roll and place the omelet onto a plate making a
slit on top. Garnish with a piece of parsley and desired fruit.

QUICHE-SHAKIRA-BETTER WAY

Six ounce Swiss or cheddar cheese shredded
¼ cup turkey or beef bacon diced and cooked or bacon of choice
Six eggs
5 fl. Ounce Heavy cream
Salt and white pepper (Optional)
One teaspoon nutmeg (Optional)
Prepared pie shell (recipe page 185)

Combine the milk, cheese, eggs and optional spices, making a custard. Stir
in the meat. Render mixture into the pie shell. Bake at 350 ° F for 25
minutes or until eggs or set.

AUNT ELLEN OLD FOLK REAL SAUSAGE RECIPE

Two pounds of beef ground meat or meat of your choice
Two medium onions sautéed in olive oil
Four cloves garlic
Two teaspoon marjoram
Two teaspoon thyme
Two teaspoon sage
One teaspoon sorrel finely chopped
Two teaspoon rosemary
Two teaspoon oregano ground
One teaspoon black pepper
¼ teaspoon nutmeg
One tablespoon brown sugar
¼ cup butter
Two tablespoons olive oil
¼ cup beef stock
¼ cup whole grain flour
One teaspoon salt

Directions for making sausage is noted in the Appendix section under Making Your Own Sausage, page 139. Feel free to experiment with different meat choices.

SCRAMBLE EGGS EASY PEA-SY

Six large whole eggs
¼ cup milk
Three tablespoons margarine
Salt (Optional)
Dash ground black pepper
One cup green peas
One small red bell pepper (seeded and ribs taken out)
Two shallots minced

In a skillet sauté peas, pepper and shallots. Sauté until the shallots are translucent. Remove from the pan and set aside. In large mixing bowl, beat the eggs with a wire whisk. In the same pan used for the peas, pour half of the eggs, and let them cook without stirring until the bottom and edges are set. Remove from heat and add half of the pea mixture. Pour ¼ eggs mixture in skillet cook until eggs set do not stir. Cook until the mixture begins to set on the bottom and around the edges. Remove from heat and add portions of the sautéed peas, bell pepper, shallots on top of egg layer portioned two eggs at a time. Fold eggs from corner to corner in a rolling manner.

RED MEAT & RABBIT

CURRIED LAMB CHOP DINNER

Six lamb chops
½ cup celery
One teaspoon marjoram
One teaspoon sage
One teaspoon thyme
One tablespoon curry powder
Salt and pepper…your discretion
One cup heavy cream
¼ cup onions
One tablespoon cornstarch
½ cup olive oil
Four cloves garlic
One bunch collard greens (cooked)
¼ cup chicken stock
Three cups pinto beans cooked

In a cast iron skillet with ¼ cup olive oil, brown lamb chops on each side. Add celery, onions, garlic, and all spices. Sauté until tender and fragrant. Mix cornstarch with vegetable stock and pour over lamb chops. Simmer for 35 minutes. Serve with collard greens, pinto beans and cornbread.

SMOKED RIBS

Three pounds of beef or pork ribs
Three cups Bemjag seasoning (recipe page 76)
Three cups apple cider vinegar
4-5 pounds of oak wood

Mix seasoning and vinegar. Pour of ribs and marinate for 8 hours or overnight. Smoke ribs for 15 hours @ 150-225 ° F.

SMOKED BRISKET

Sixteen pounds beef brisket
Three cups Bemjag seasoning (recipe page 76)
Three cups apple cider vinegar
4-5 pounds of oak wood

Trim excess fat from the meat. Mix seasoning and vinegar. Pour over brisket and marinate for 1 hour. Smoke meat for 12-16 hours @ 150-225 ° F.

SMOTHERED SIRLOIN STEAK WITH CHEDDAR CHEESE & MUSHROOMS

Two nicely cut sirloin steaks
Four garlic cloves minced
Four medium size shallots minced
½ cup cheddar cheese
½ cup beef stock
¼ cup brown sugar
¼ cup cornstarch
Two tablespoon butter, olive oil
One teaspoon cider vinegar
One teaspoon Worcestershire sauce
One teaspoon lemon juice.
½ teaspoon ground pepper

In a cast iron skillet heat oil. Sear sirloin on both sides until brownish. Add garlic and onions, sauté until translucent. Meanwhile cream together cheese, butter, Worcestershire sauce and brown sugar. Spread cheese mixture on sirloins. Add beef stock and cornstarch mixture. Simmer for 30 minutes until tender.

SOUTHERN VEAL LOAF

Two pounds veal shank ground
Two packed cups shredded parsnips
Three shallots minced
½ cups mushrooms
One cup of dried biscuits crumbs
Salt and pepper ...your discretion
¼ cup tomato sauce
One cup heavy cream

In a mixing bowl, blend veal, biscuits crumbs, parsnips, shallots, tomato
sauce, mushrooms, and heavy cream. Render to bake dish of your choice.
Bake at 350 ° F for 70 minutes.

LIVER & ONIONS

Two pounds calf liver, sliced
Three medium onions, sliced
Four cloves garlic minced
¼ cup olive oil
¼ cup flour
Two cups beef stock
One teaspoon sage
One teaspoon marjoram
Salt and pepper to taste

Heat olive oil in a skillet. Sear liver on both sides. Add the garlic, onion,
and spices, cook for five minutes. Add the flour and beef stock to the
skillet. Stir well and reduce the heat. Simmer for 30 minutes.

AUNT MAUZIA VEAL STAY-OVER

One pound veal cubed and cut ¼ inches
Eight ounces green lima beans
One tomato
One small onion
Two cloves garlic minced
½ cup tomatoes paste
Two cups beef stock
½ cup olive oil
½ cup white grape juice

In saucepan, sauté veal in olive oil. Sear meat on all sides. Add garlic, onions, and remaining ingredients all but beans. Deglaze the pan with white grape juice. Cook for 35 minutes. Ease veal to side of the saucepan and add the beans. Sauté and cover for an additional 15 minutes over medium heat. Serve tender veal and crunchy beans over warmed rice.

SPAGHETTI SQUASH W/ MEATBALLS & ALMOND BUTTER

Two pounds ground beef
½ cup almond butter
One medium onion, diced
One medium red bell pepper, diced
Two cloves garlic
½ cup butter
One cup chicken stock
One quart water
½ cup cream
¼ cup flour
¼ cup olive oil
¼ teaspoon cinnamon
¼ teaspoon allspice
½ teaspoon white pepper
One teaspoon salt

In a saucepan, sauté the onion, bell pepper and garlic until onion is translucent. In a mixing bowl render ground beef with sautéed vegetables, ½ teaspoon pepper and ½ teaspoon salt and ½ teaspoon allspice. Form meat into balls. Place in a saucepan cook twenty minutes over medium heat in own fat. Render oil, flour, ½ teaspoon salt and butter in a skillet making a roux. Add allspice, almond butter, cream and chicken stock. Stir until smooth. In a medium saucepot with one quart of water bring to a boil. Add spaghetti squash. Cook for 15 minutes and submerse in cold water stopping the cooking process. Cut the spaghetti squash in half scoop out the flesh place on a platter with meat balls, add cream sauce conservatively. Garnish with kale.

LAMB MEATBALLS W/ ALMOND BUTTER

1 ½ ground lamb
Two teaspoons black cumin
Two teaspoon dried basil
One teaspoon coriander
½ cup tomato paste
Two teaspoon allspice
¼ cup olive oil
Two teaspoons light butter
One medium onion diced
½ cup almond butter

In a saucepan heat oil and butter. Add onions and spices, cook until onions are translucent. Remove from heat. In a mixing bowl place ground lamb, tomato paste, almond butter, onion, and spices. Mix and roll into balls. Render them to a saucepan with the olive oil. Cook until done, approximately 20 minutes.

CABBAGE & BEEF

One medium cabbage
Eight cubes of beef from shank 1/8-inch slices
One medium onion, sliced
¼ cup of butter
¼ cup beef broth
Two tablespoon water
Two chopped green chili peppers
One tablespoon of brown sugar

Wash cabbage thoroughly and tear into small pieces. Render all ingredients into a medium sauce pot. Bring to steam, then simmer in its juices, for 45 minutes. Place shank meat in a saucepan with beef broth. Cover saucepot tightly with aluminum foil and bake for one hour at375 ° F. Remove from oven and add to cabbage.

CABBAGE & BEEF W/ CHERRY PEPPERS

One medium cabbage pick leaf apart
One small onion, sliced
½ teaspoon cinnamon
¾ teaspoon apple cider
¼ cup of grapeseed oil
Three whole okra, chopped
Two cups of cherry pepper
Eight pieces of cube ½ inch beef cooked
¼ cup of water

Heat oil in saucepan. Add cabbage, beef, okra, water, cinnamon, and peppers. Bring to a slight boil. Reduce heat and simmer for 25 minutes. Remove and serve over rice.

BLACK BEAN & BRISKET

Six pounds brisket
Three cups cooked black beans
½ cup Bemjag seasoning (recipe page 76)
One cup beef broth

Trim excess fat from brisket and rub seasoning all over. Add seasoned meat to a deep baking dish with ½ cup of beef broth. Cover tightly with foil and cook for 4 hours in a 275 °F oven. While that is cooking add beans and remaining broth to a blender. Blend until smooth. Add mixture to the brisket and cook uncovered for 20 minutes. Serve with rice.

MUSTARD GREENS W/ BEEF TIPS

Eight pieces cubed 1/8-inch chuck beef
Two bunches of mustard greens
Three shallots minced
One medium sweet onion
Three cloves garlic
Four medium size shallots diced
Two cups of beef broth
¼ cup of olive oil
One tablespoon apple cider
¼ teaspoon cayenne

Wash greens and beef in cold water. Place greens in medium pot. Cook for 1 hour 45 minutes. In saucepan heat oil to 350 ° F and place kosher beef in pan. Adjust heat to a simmer. Season the meat with shallots, sweet onion, garlic cayenne and apple cider. Cook 45 minutes until tender. Add beef to greens.

STEWED RED POTATOES - LAMB CHOPS

Five pounds of small – Pontiac- type red potatoes
Eight small cut lamb chops, 1/16 inch
Two teaspoons of rosemary leave
One small yellow bell pepper, sliced
One small red bell pepper, sliced
One teaspoon nutmeg
Two teaspoon allspice
¼ cup olive oil

Heat oil in saucepan. Submerge chops in olive oil. Reduce heat to a simmer
and cook for 15 minutes until done. Peel and wash potatoes. Place potatoes
in boiling salted water in medium saucepot. Cook until tender. Add
peppers cook 5 minutes, arrange lamb chops on platter garnish with green
onions.

BEEF POLLI POP CRISP

Four pounds beef sausage
One quart olive oil
One cup flour
One cup corn meal
½ cup baking powder
½ cup Bemjag seasoning (recipe page 76)

In a deep fryer add olive oil and heat to 350 °F. In the meantime, slice
sausage into ¼ rounds. Mix flour, corn meal, baking powder and
seasoning into a dish. Dredge sausage into the flour mixture until coated
well all over. Place into the fryer and cook until sausage floats to the top.
Drain on paper towel lined dish.

STUFFED CURVENECK SQUASH W/ GROUND BEEF

Eight curveneck yellow squash
One pounds ground beef
One cup chopped snow peas
One cup finely chopped carrot top
Salt and pepper to taste

In a saucepan cook ground beef for until done. Place carrot tops and chopped snow peas in skillet with oil. Cook until tender. Add ground beef to the vegetable mixture. Cut the squash horizontally. Remove the flesh and add to the beef mixture. Cook for 20 minutes until the flesh is tender. Stuff the squash with mixture.

OLE STYLE CALVES 'LIVER W/ ONIONS

Two pounds sliced calves' liver
Three medium onions sliced one-eighth inch thick
Four cloves garlic minced
¼ cup of olive oil
¼ cup flour
Two cups beef stock
One teaspoon sage
One teaspoon marjoram
Salt, pepper (Optional)

Place liver in frying pan with ¼ cup olive oil and ¼ cup flour. sear on both sides, adding garlic and spices. Cook for 20 minutes then add onion and beef stock. Reduce heat, stir, and simmer for 15 minutes. Onions should be tender and crunchy.

FARM RAISED VENISON BRAISED

¾ rack of venison cut in quarter pieces
½ cup olive oil
1/8 cup vegetable stock
One medium onion
Four cloves garlic minced
1/8 cup heavy cream
¼ cup flour
Salt and pepper… (Optional)

In a heavy skillet add olive oil. Place venison in hot skillet and cook for
10 minutes. This meat is especially mild, and tender. It does not require
abundant heat. Sear heavily on both sides, adding 1/8 cup vegetable stock.
Transfer to a tightly covered casserole dish and slide in a preheated 250 ° F
oven. Braise for 25 minutes or until tender. In a separate skillet add ¼ olive
oil, flour, onions, garlic and heavy cream. Stir and mix well. Add to
blender, mix until smooth and creamy. When rack of venison is done,
remove and add the cream sauce. Garnish with tarragon.

BLACK BEANS & CORNED BEEF

Two inch thick brisket with a streak of fat
½ gallon water (beef broth)
One pounds of black beans (presoaked)
One medium onion
One tablespoon honey
1 tablespoon brown sugar
¼ cup olive oil
Salt and pepper (Optional)

Place all ingredients in medium pot. Cook on high heat for 35 minutes.
Reduce heat and simmer for 3 hours 25 minutes.

SMOKED RABBIT

3-4 pounds jack rabbit, cleaned
Four cups apple cider vinegar
Three ounces of cold smoked seasoning (recipe page 76)

Mix seasoning and vinegar. Pour on meat and marinate for 1 hour. Smoke
for 3 -4 hours @ 150-225 ° F.

BUTTER BEANS W/ GROUND BEEF

¼ cup ground beef
One pounds of butter beans (presoaked)
½ gallon of beef stock
¼ cup honey
One medium onion
Four garlic gloves finely diced
½ tablespoon cardamom
¼ cup of grapeseed oil
 Salt and pepper (Optional)

Place ground beef, onion, and garlic in saucepan cook 15 minutes. In a
medium saucepot add butter beans to boiling stock. Cook for 90 minutes
on high heat. Remove and add ground beef mixture.

STUFFED BELL PEPPERS W/ GROUND BEEF

One pounds ground beef lean (cooked)
¼ cup olive oil
1 large onion
4 gloves garlic diced
One teaspoon cumin
½ teaspoon cardamom
½ tablespoon chili powder
Eight bell peppers seeded

Place ground beef and spices in skillet. Cook until beef is no longer pink.
Remove top, seeds, and ribs from peppers. Stuff with ground beef. Bake at
350 ° F for 40 minutes.

SMOKED LAMB SHOULDER

Six pounds of lamb shoulder
Eight garlic cloves, minced
Eight shallots, minced
Two tablespoons Bemjag seasoning (recipe page 76)
¼ cup mint jelly
Two ounces cold smoked seasoning (recipe page 76)

Mix above ingredients minus lamb into a bowl. Rub mixture over the
meat. With butcher's twine, roll meat tightly. Let marinate for 30 minutes.
Smoke for 6-8 hours at 225 ° F.

FARM VENISON SIMMERED

Two pounds of venison cut into small pieces
½ cup of olive oil
¼ cup vegetable stock
One medium onion
Four garlic cloves, minced
½ cup heavy cream
¼ cup flour
Salt and pepper to taste

Heat a heavy cast iron skillet with olive oil. Place the venison in the hot skillet, cook for 10 minutes. This meat is especially mild and tender and does not require abundant heat. Sear heavily on each side adding ¼ cup of vegetable stock. In a separate skillet at ¼ cup olive oil and flour to make a roux. Add the onions, garlic and heavy cream. Stir well. Add this sauce to the seared meat and cook on low heat for 45 minutes.

EGGPLANT & BEEF

One medium eggplant
Six pound beef brisket
½ cup flour
One cup sliced onions
Four garlic gloves
¼ cup annatto
One cup beef stock

Wash and slice eggplant. Set aside. Prepare brisket. In a large casserole dish place beef and seasonings into preheated 300 ° F oven. Cook for 3 hours or until tender. Remove from the oven and pour juices into a blender. Blend until smooth and pour back into the casserole dish adding the eggplant. Cook for 20 minutes or until eggplant is slightly tender.

ANCHO DRIED PEPPERS STUFFED W/ REFRIED BEANS & CHEESE

One pound pinto beans (presoaked)
½ gallon beef broth
Ten ancho dried peppers
One medium onion
Two cloves of garlic finely chopped
¼ teaspoon chili powder
Three tablespoon butter
Sixteen ounces grated cheese
Two tablespoons brown sugar

Place beans in medium pot. Add onion, garlic, chili powder, brown sugar, butter and beef broth. Bring to a rolling boil, reduce heat. Simmer for 4 hours. Remove beans from stove top and mix until lumpy. Stuff the peppers with the beans and cheese. Place in the oven until cheese is melted.

STUFFED POBLANO PEPPERS & REMIXED BEEF

One pound ground beef
Eight ounces cheddar cheese
Ten poblano peppers
¼ cup olive oil
One teaspoon allspice
One teaspoon cardamom
One teaspoon cinnamon

Place ground beef and spices in saucepot with hot oil. Reduce heat and cook for 45 minutes, or until tender. Remove from heat. Stir and mix meat until slightly lumpy. Cut open the peppers, stuff with spiced beef. Sprinkle with cheese. Serve with radish leaves and spinach.

SOUTHERN LAND LAMB ROAST

Three pound lamb roast
½ cup olive oil
Two teaspoon rosemary
One teaspoon cardamom
One teaspoon allspice
One teaspoon white pepper
Two teaspoon brown sugar
One tablespoon brown sugar
¼ cup vegetable soup base

Place roast in saucepan with olive oil. Sear all sides until dark brown.
Blend herbs and spices with vegetable base making a wet rub. Rub roast
on all sides. Place in baking dish. Set oven at 350 ° F. Bake for 1 hour or
until desired doneness. Add salt if desired.

OVEN BARBEQUE LAMB

Twelve lamb chops
Eight ounces cold smoked seasoning (recipe page 76)
One cup barbeque sauce
½ cup vegetable soup base

Marinade lamb with soup base. Place lamb chops on rack in baking dish
sprinkle seasoning and barbeque sauce on lamb. Bake 300 ° F for 1 hour.

PAN FRIED RABBIT W/ CREAM GRAVY

One 2-pound rabbit cut in six pieces
½ cup heavy cream
¼ teaspoon thyme
¼ teaspoon sage
¼ teaspoon rosemary
¼ teaspoon marjoram
¼ tablespoon brown sugar
¼ tablespoon flour
¼ teaspoon apple cider vinegar
¼ cup olive oil
½ cup chicken stock
Salt and pepper (Optional)

Season the rabbit with the spices and dredge into the flour. In a heavy cast iron skillet saturated with one tablespoon olive oil render floured seasoned rabbit. Seared on both sides for 10 minutes. In a blender add heavy cream, olive oil and chicken stock. Puree until smooth then yield to skillet. Simmer for 25 minutes or until desired tenderness.

SMOTHERED LAMB CHOPS

Twelve lamb chops
¼ cup olive oil
½ cup flour
Two cups vegetable stock
One teaspoon white pepper
Salt and pepper to taste

In a saucepan heat oil until hot. Place chops in hot oil and fry until brownish. Add flour making a roux. Add stock and simmer for 20 minutes.

AUNT ELLEN POT ROAST

Four pounds beef from round
¼ cup flour
One gallon water
Two cups Joanna Marie mix (recipe page 77)
Two bay leaves
Two gloves
¼ cup vegetable oil
¼ cup brown sugar
Salt and pepper to taste

In a cast iron pot, brown beef on all sides. Add flour. Mix until dark brown in color. Add water. Cook on high heat for 90 minutes. Simmer until mixture become bubbly and meat is tender.

TEXAS CHUCK ROAST W/ MASHED VEGETABLES

Four pounds chuck roast cubed in ¼ -inch pieces
Two pounds carrots cut in large pieces
Three large onions
Four large potatoes
½ cup butter
One quart of beef stock
Salt and pepper (Optional)

Wash and peel all vegetables. Cut onion into large pieces. In a large skillet heat butter and quickly add meat. Sear on all sides. Reduce heat and add beef stock. Simmer for one hour and the vegetables. Cook for 30 minutes until ready for mashing. Add the remaining ingredients. Stir and whip the vegetables into a smooth but stiff product. Using a 3 inch scoop, place a portion of mash vegetables and chuck roast on serving plate.

BRAISED RABBIT W/ MUSHROOMS

One 3-pound rabbit cut in eight pieces
¼ cup olive oil
¼ teaspoon marjoram
¼ teaspoon thyme
¼ teaspoon sage
¼ teaspoon rosemary
One cup shiitake mushrooms
One tablespoon chicken stock

Brown rabbit in skillet with olive oil. Place rabbit in a saucepan and add one tablespoon chicken stock, barely covering the bottom of the pan. Render all eight pieces of rabbit to the sauce dish cover tightly and braise at 200 ° F for 2 hours. In a saucepan sauté mushrooms with remaining spices. Render to a platter and garnish with carrot tops.

SWEET & SMOKEY VEAL CUTLETS

Four veal cutlets cut ½ inch thick
Three tablespoons light butter
Three shallots minced
Two cloves garlic
¼ cup olive oil
One tablespoon whole wheat flour
¼ cup cold smoked seasoning (recipe page 76)
¼ cup honey
One tablespoon dill weed
¼ cup beef stock
½ cup crushed pineapple
¼ cup pineapple juice
One teaspoon allspice
Salt and pepper (Optional)

Rub cold smoked seasoning vigorously into veal, set aside. In a saucepan heat olive oil and butter. Sear seasoned veal cutlets, constantly turning them on each side for 15 minutes. Remove meat from the pan and add the onions, garlic, and flour. Stir well, then add beef stock, pineapple juice and honey. Simmer 3 minutes. Place meat back into the pan.

SWEET & SAVORY PIES

OLE FASHION PIE DOUGH

Four cups enriched flour
One cup whole wheat flour
Two cups vegetable shortening
One teaspoon baking powder
One teaspoon brown sugar
One tablespoon vinegar
One egg beaten
One tablespoon cold water
Two tablespoon cold milk

In a mixing bowl, mix flour, shortening, baking powder, sugar forming a pea like appearance. Blend until it resembles coarse meal. Add the egg, milk and water to the mixture. Knead and roll the dough, testing for dryness in the dough, if the dough is too dry add more milk or cold water and continue to knead the dough is in the right consistency. Roll the dough on a floured surface. Place into pie shape or tart form.

BASIC HOME DOUGH

3 ½ cups flour
One teaspoon salt
¼ cup cane sugar
Two cups vegetable shortening
One cup cold milk
Two ounces dry yeast

In a mixing bowl combine flour, salt sugar and milk. Mix well. Add the shortening a few tablespoons at a time until the mixture is course.

BUTTERED PASTRY DOUGH

2½ cups enriched flour
½ cup whole wheat flour
½ teaspoon salt
One cup butter... cut in small parts
Four tablespoon cold milk
Four tablespoon ice water
One tablespoon vinegar

Blend flour and butter until mixture resemble course meal. Add milk and water and knead dough until it resembles a flat disk. Dust dough with flour and roll with rolling pen to the desired shape or circle.

CHERRY BERRY PIE

Two cups Bing cherries or the cherries of your choice
Two cups granulated sugar
Three tablespoons cornstarch
½ cup milk
One tablespoon heavy cream (Optional)
You will need a top and bottom crust (recipe page 124 or 125)

In a medium bowl combine sugar, cherries, milk and cornstarch making certain the cornstarch is not lumpy. Render filling to prepared bottom crust arranging fruit slightly in the center. Brush edge of pastry with a dab of water. Roll the prepared top crust on a baker rolling pen and place on top of prepared pie plate. Brush top with cream and sprinkle with sugar. Cut vents in top of pie to release steam. Place pie on baking sheet and bake at 350 ° F for 60 minutes.

WATERMELON-O-RIND PIE

One cups of mashed watermelon rind
Three tablespoons flour
Sixteen ounces sugar
One tablespoon allspice
Dash nutmeg
Pinch cream of tarter
One teaspoon cinnamon
One tablespoon vanilla
Four eggs one separated from yolk
½ cup butter
Eight ounces whole milk
Twelve ounces cream milk
Two prepared pie shells (recipe page 124 or 125)

Render watermelon rind, sugar, three whole eggs and one egg yolk, butter, flour, spices in a mixing bowl. Blend ingredients for 30 minutes on low speed. With mixer in off position, add milk and resume at a moderate speed for about 20 minutes. In another bowl, crack egg and separate the yolk from the white, add the cream of tartar to the egg white and beat at a high rate of speed until peaks are formed combine and fold in with the batter. In prepared deep-dish pan bake at 250 ° F for 50 minutes. Increase heat to 350 ° F for 15 minutes. Yield two 9-inch-deep dish pies. Yummy, delicious

GEORGIA SWEET POTATO PIE

2 ¼ cups mashed sweet potatoes
One teaspoon ginger
One teaspoon cinnamon
One teaspoon allspice
¼ teaspoon nutmeg
Pinch of cream of tarter
Two cups whole milk
One cup heavy cream
1 ½ tablespoons vanilla extract
One teaspoon lemon grated
One tablespoon flour
Four eggs… separate one egg white from the yolk
One cup butter
Two tablespoon grated lemon peel
¼ cup lemon juice
Prepared pie crust (recipe page 124)

In a large bowl combine ingredient: sweet potatoes butter, eggs, flour, and spices. Mix on moderate speed for 20 minutes. Add milk, heavy cream and vanilla. Blend for another 20 minutes at a low speed. Place the separated egg white and cream of tartar in another bowl. Mix at a high speed until peaks form then fold mix into sweet potato batter. Pour batter into prepared deep-dish pie shells. Bake at 350 ° F for 55 minutes.

PEACH CHEESY PIE

Six cups ripe pitted peaches
One cup of melted cheddar cheese
One cup sugar
½ cup butter
¼ cup cornstarch
One teaspoon cinnamon
¼ teaspoon nutmeg
½ cup peach juice
Prepared pie crust (recipe page 124 or 125)

Blend peaches, sugar, butter, spices. Mix ½ cup peach juice, with
cornstarch. Fold in with the peach mix, be sure it is not lumpy. Pour in
prepared pie shell. Roll prepared top crust over and cut slits in top to
eliminate steam. Bake at 350 ° F for 55 minutes. Remove from oven and
pour melted cheese on top. Slide back into oven and bake for 5 minutes
until brownish on top.

AUTUMN PECAN PIE

Two cups pecan halves, reserving ¼ cup
Three eggs
One teaspoon Vanilla extract
One cup light corn syrup
One cup packed light brown sugar
½ cup butter melted
One tablespoon flour
One deep dish pie shell (recipe page 124)

In a large bowl gently fold in sugar, butter and flour until smooth. Blend in
corn syrup, vanilla and eggs. Stir in pecans halves. Render to prepared
crust. Bake in oven for 60 minutes at 325 ° F. Sprinkle crushed pecans on
top bake 2 minutes. Remove and cool.

CHERRY APPLE PEAR PIE

Five apples peeled seeds removed and thinly sliced
Two cups pitted sweet cherries
One cup pears peel and seeded
1 ½ cups granulated sugar
Four tablespoons cornstarch
One teaspoon vanilla extract
One teaspoon cinnamon
Prepared pie crust (recipe page 125)

Roll out dough for a 9-inch pie dusting the work area with flour to keep
the dough from sticking. Press dough in pie pan, crimping the edges for a
decorative appearance. In a mixing bowl combine the fruit, cinnamon,
sugar, cornstarch, and vanilla. Place the batter into crust. Bake at 350 ° F for
55 minutes. Remove from oven. Place strips of prepared dough attractively
on top of pie. Return pie to oven and continue to bake for an additional 40
minutes or until the strips are nicely browned.

MANGO PIE

5 ½ cups mangos peel and pitted
One cup granulated sugar
Four tablespoons cornstarch
Two tablespoons freshly squeezed lime juice
¼ cup mango juice
One tablespoon butter
Two prepared pie crusts (recipe page 125)

Combine mangos with sugar, lime juice and butter. Blend cornstarch with
mangos making sure cornstarch is smooth without lumps. Render filling to
prepared bottom crust right in the center of pie. Brush edge of pie with a
dab of water. With a rolling pin, roll the top piece of the pastry onto the
pan. Cut slits in top of pie to provide for steam to escape. Bake at 350 ° F 55
minutes. Remove, brush with cream and sugar, and return pie to oven for
5 minutes or until golden brown.

TURKEY CHICKEN BEEF VEGETABLE POTPIE

¼ cup turkey breast diced
¼ cup beef from shank diced
¼ cup chicken breast diced
¼ cup butter
¼ tablespoon cornstarch
½ cup vegetable stock
One teaspoon onion minced
One teaspoon garlic minced
One teaspoon marjoram
One teaspoon sage
One teaspoon thyme
One celery rib, chopped
One tablespoon corn
One tablespoon green peas
One tablespoon red bell pepper
Salt.... (Optional)
Two prepared pie crusts (recipe page 125)

In a skillet sauté the vegetables, chicken, beef, turkey, spices in butter. Mix the cornstarch with vegetable stock. Add to the skillet with the vegetable and meat mixture and cook for 15 minutes. With prepared bottom pie crust render the mixture to the center of bottom crust spreading the filling. With a rolling pin roll the top pie crust on to the pie plate. Brush a dab of water around the edge of pie plate to guard against leaks. Cut slits in top of pie to allow for steam to escape. Bake at 350 ° F for 45 minutes.

CHICKEN POTPIE

One cup chicken diced
¼ cup corn
¼ cup peas
One cup of carrots
One tablespoon flour
¼ cup light butter
½ cup chicken stock
One teaspoon sage
One teaspoon thyme
One teaspoon marjoram
Salt and pepper... (Optional)

Sauté chicken with one tablespoon butter until tender. Remove chicken from pan. Place one tablespoon butter and spices in saucepan. Add flour and stir until golden in color. Render chicken stock and vegetables to the roux. With a prepared bottom crust add the filling and a dab of water around the edges to ensure seal. Add the top crust by rolling the top crust with a rolling pin on the pie plate after crimping the edges of the pie. Cut slits on top of pie to ensure steam to escape. Bake at 350 ° F for 55 minutes.

AUNT GERTHA LEE'S- CHOCOLATE PIE

Six ounces semi- yolks sweet chocolate pieces
One teaspoon vanilla extract
Two whole eggs
Two egg whites
1 ¼ cups heavy cream
Two   tablespoon chocolate chips
One whole egg
One deep-dish pie shell, baked

Melt chocolate and remove from heat. Beat in whole egg and egg yolk one
at a time. In a separate mixing bowl, beat egg whites until they form peaks.
Whip ¼ cup of heavy cream into another mixing bowl. Fold egg whites
into chocolate mixture then add cream. Delicately, pour into baked pie
shell. Whip remaining ¼ cream and garnish pie with chocolate chip pieces
and cream; refrigerate.

BEAN PIE

One cup cooked white beans
Two tablespoons flour
½ cup softened butter
One cup whole milk
12 oz can condensed milk
Four eggs
One tablespoon vanilla
One tablespoon allspice
¼ teaspoon nutmeg
Two prepared deep-dish pie shells (recipe page 124)

Beat eggs in a mixer until peaks form. Set aside. Mix sugar and butter
together until creamy. Add spices, bean, flour, and blended eggs. Mix well.
Pour pie batter into shells and bake at 350 °F for 45-60 minutes.

APPENDIX

CULTIVATING A HOME-GROWN GARDEN

Now you are embarking on a venture that will give you much satisfaction. First select a suitable site in your yard a place that takes plenty of sunlight. The tools that you will need are: Sharpshooter shovel with a round head, flat head shovel, big tooth Iron Rake, and a Soil Tiller, in preparing a modest size garden (10x25 ft.) be sure that you have no tree roots. With a soil tiller, till the soil at least three times. Make the soil soft as possible and pliable when breaking it down with an Aggie (garden hoe). After a considerable time of cultivating and removing all foreign debris and the earth is like coarse sand, arrange the rows 1x10 ft for planting. Select your seeds and choose your vegetables that you will plant. There is a REASON for the SEASON. For that, consult your farmer's almanac for the time of planting. Consider vegetables that are leafy and can be grown in partial shade. However, the one that bears fruit can be grown in direct sunlight. As an added security, build a fence around your garden to keep out dogs, cats, and rabbits. Conversely, a second fence can be used as a trellis for tomatoes, peas, beans, and other vegetables that need support.

In certain parts of the world there are rodents that are very pesky. They can be kept out of your garden with a self-made electrical buffer surrounding the fence. Do not grow vegetables vines on this fence the electricity will deteriorate them. This is the first fence about three feet from the second fence that accommodates the trellis.

The buffer has an electrical charge running through it. It has strands of thick gauges of wire stretched between twelve small wooden posts surrounding a 10 x 25-foot garden. The charge can be regulated through an electrical panel. The wire and panel can be bought at any feed and grain store.

A good drainage system is essential and necessary for a successful garden. Protect your garden with a proper drainage system be sure it is on high ground and not subject to overflow from surrounding ditches and ponds that could drain into your garden. If high ground is not available, you must dig trenches or water escape routes surrounding your GARDEN.

In proper seasons protect your vegetation from frost with a heavy cloth canvas.

To further protect your invested interest, supply your garden with ladybugs. They are predators that eat many aphids that suck the juices of plants. They may eat up to 10,000 aphids in a lifetime. This greatly reduces the population of harmful insects that will otherwise destroy your plants and, they will eliminate the use of harmful pesticides. Moreover, the ladybugs are very beautiful creatures that lend beauty to your landscape and garden as well. They are decked with orange and a red shell with black dots. This bug is a work of art. The Lance wing bug resembles a small alligator and is very ferocious feeders and they consume a variety of small insects, moths, leafhoppers caterpillars, mites' psyllids, mealy bugs, aphids, whiteflies and thrips, these bugs are awesome.

The nematode is also parasitic they are helpful in killing root weevils, cutworms, cabbage root maggots, lawn grubs, Turf webworms, peach tree Boers, Iris Boers, and flea beetle larvae. The Nematodes spend their entire life in the soil killing larvae of pest.

Be sure to not overload the Garden with too many nematodes because they can upset the balance of predators in the garden.

FRUITS

A fruit is a produce that develops from a flowering plant or is a pulpy edible product of a plant, vine, or tree and has one or more seeds. Fruits come in many varieties and categories to name a few: figs, bananas pomegranate, kiwis Melons, grapes, oranges, apples, and grapefruit. The species of beans eggplant and many seeded peppers are fruits. Fruits can be called by several names depending on the regions or countries, which they are grown or developed.

VEGETABLES

Vegetable nutrients are found just below the skin. To ensure the vitamins and minerals stays intact wash them under cold water with a fine soft brush. Indigestible substances such as cellulose, and lignin, known as fiber, supply much of the physiology of the vegetable. Be aware that vegetables lose nutrients to the air or to any liquid, which they can soak. The color of the vegetable is an indicator of the type of nutrients it supplies green leafy vegetables (spinach, chard (which is a particularly good source of foliate), kale, beetroot leaves is known to supply vitamin C and Iron. They are also known to be a detoxifier because of their chlorophyll content.
Carrots, sweet potatoes, pumpkins, squash, are rich in beta-carotene, a forerunner of vitamin A...., although tomatoes come in a variety of colors: Red, green, yellow, they all supply lycopene a powerful antioxidant

MAKING YOUR OWN SAUSAGE

Sausages are quite easy and simple to make. The same principle applies today as it did hundreds of years ago. To make sausages you will need a meat, grinder, meat grinder blades your choice to choose from: ½ hole,3/8 hole, or ¼ hole a meat grinder plate disc, tamper or meat pusher, a sausage stuffer, sharp knives, meat tamper or meat pusher, bowls. Weight scales, temperature gauge, measuring spoons. We shall focus on the fresh sausage that has not been cured or smoked or chemicals have not been added such as sodium nitrite. Prepare meat using a weight scale from your choice of meat, cut the meat in one-eighth-inch cubes. Add your cubed meat(you can use meat from any part of an animal carcass) to a grinder if you do not have a grinder very sharp knives will be sufficient, place the meat on a cutting board and chop the meat until it becomes a nice ground and then add the ground meat into a bowl and mix well with your favorite spices add the ground meat to the meat grinder(a slow grind please) or hand chop once more, and with a portion scoop dip a bit of meat from the bowl then force the meat into the sausage stuffer or nozzle by extruding the meat into the casing or just receive the meat by hand from the sausage stuffer or nozzle and fashion the meat into a desired rolled sausage or into the casing . Render Sausage on a baking sheet, brushed lightly with olive oil and bake at 325 ° F. Insert a Temperature Gauge into the sausage when the temperature reaches 172 ° F internally. At this temperature, the sausage is done. Do not exceed this temperature because the sausage will become dry and crumbly.

PASTRIES

Pastries is a food product made from flour, milk, eggs, water, sugar and oil. This will result in a high content of sugar and fat and is not conducive to weight conscious persons. Pastries come in delicious items such as cakes, pies, tarts, and donuts. In this book you shall be introduced to the world-famous bean pie.

Be aware that bread flour and cake flour are not the same. In making cakes and other pastries know that there is a difference in shortening and butter. During experimentation, you shall learn to make adjustments. Therefore, the baking experience would be successful and consistent.

HOW TO BUILD A HOME SMOKER

Materials needed:
Refrigerator
Hole saw, one" and four" diameters
30-gallon drum
A partial hose from a clothes dryer
Sealant or coating used by dentist

To get started, select a clear spot in your yard away from trees and tall grassy areas. Build a wood pile and circle it with water, wet the area good. Initiate the fire burning process. Place the refrigerator on the wood pile. Burn until the enamel or coating is burned completely off. Let it cool for a day or so. Cut a four" holes in the drum and the refrigerator. Take the dryer hose and secure it to the refrigerator and drum. Make certain there are no leaks. Use the sealant around the perimeter inside the door prohibiting smoke from escaping. Cut a one" hole at the top of the refrigerator creating a smoke escape route. Cut another one" hole in the door inserting a thermometer.

HINTS, TIPS AND OBSERVATIONS

1. Always wash hands with soapy water and scrub with nail brush before preparing meals.
2. Wash fruits and vegetables, fish and meats under cold running water.
3. To keep green in vegetables, boil ten minutes with a dash of baking soda, douse in ice cold water stopping the cooking process.
4. Cooking can be an art form following techniques will make a more productive experience.
5. Always keep hot foods hot and cold foods cold.
6. Foods at warmest temperatures offer strong tastes.
7. Food with components of sweetness pairs well with sweet natural juices to void of additives.
8. Never add fresh foods to leftover food.
9. Always reheat foods to at least 165. °F.
10. Temperature danger zones start at 41 °F. 95 °C and ends at 135 °F (57 °C) Suggested by the FDA model food code.
11. Food that is started from scratch: All ethnic American cuisine.
12. Despite making roux, adding stock it will surely thicken up.
13. When removing meat from the shank bone or any bone, with a knife, cut parallel to the bone.
14. Great home cooking comes from the heart.
15. Home cooks know it takes more than a recipe to cook a meal, it takes love from the heart and appreciation and respect and willingness for experimentation.

16. Always cook game birds medium rare and cover with strips of fat. If cooked well done the become dry and stringy.
17. Always clean mollusks and other shellfish like clams under cold running water with a brush to remove mud, sand and silt.
18. All fats are shortening in baking because it makes all wheat products; bread and cakes tender and shortens gluten strands.
19. The process of exposing foods to smoke at temperatures of 200 °F to 250 °F is called hot smoking.
20. Foods smoked at 50° F to 85°F is called cold smoking.
21. Always baste turkeys to keep moisture in the bird. Temperature should be 169 ° F, 76° C in thigh when done.
22. A proven and constant method for checking temperature in large birds like turkeys, insert the thermometer gauge at the coolest part of the bird which would be the thigh.
23. Stuffed turkeys should be cooked longer to cook the stuffing properly, which is probable cause that the meat will become overcooked.
24. Turkey meat is second to chicken meat in the United States. It has both light and dark meat and has a small amount of fat. The young turkeys are reasonable in price and can be cooked in any manner: broiled, baked, fried, stewed, roast, braised, ground, boiled. However, these cooking methods vary with the age of the turkey.
25. Wild game is traditionally very tough therefore a marinating process should be in place, red wine vinegar, herbs and bemjag seasoning.
26. When storing game, it should be wrapped well at temperatures of 41 ° F, 5 ° C.
27. Ranch raised game is much more tender than their counterparts that roam the countryside.

28. Black sea bass has a mild flavor and flaky texture. Cooking methods desired by cooks are baking and pan frying.
29. Red snapper has lean pink flesh that becomes white when cooked. It truly has a delicious, sweet flavor.
30. Mackerel are best when smoked or grilled. It has a mild flaky texture.
31. Always avoid using aluminum pots when making roux. It leaves a metallic taste.
32. Broccoli will benefit from partial cooking to cut the firmness. The woody stems are a good compliment to soups.
33. Bok choy is also known as pok choy, a southern Chinese cabbage. It is enjoyed pickled.
34. Cabbage is a quick growing and inexpensive. It is available year-round and is a southern American favorite.
35. Avocados are best when soft to the touch and very ripe. Green avocados can be left at room temperature to ripen.
36. Chayote is a food staple of South America. There are a variety of ways to prepare.

MEASUREMENTS AND CONVERSION CHART

1 oz	1/16	
16 oz	1 lb.	480 g
4 oz	¼ lb.	120 g
8 oz	½ lb.	240 g
12 oz	¾ lb.	360 g
1 cup		250 ml
¾ cup		175 ml
1 ½ teaspoon		7 ml
1 tablespoon		
¼ teaspoon		1 ml
1 teaspoon		1 ml
2 teaspoons		2 ml
3 teaspoons		5 ml
4 teaspoons	1 tablespoon	½ oz 15 ml
5 teaspoons	1/8 cup	1 oz 30 ml
6 teaspoons	¼ cup	2 oz 60 ml
7 teaspoons	2 1/3 teaspoon	1/3 cup 80 ml

¼ lb.	4 oz	½ cup	120g
8 oz	1 cup	½ lb.	240 g
16 oz	2 cups	1 lb.	480g
32 oz	4 cups	2 lb.	960g
36 oz	5 cups	2 ¼ lb.	

GLOSSARY

Acid: To make neutral; a base alkaline in a liquid solution.

Aging: A period of rest after slaughter of meat so the effects of rigor mortis shall dissipate.

Baking: A dry heat cooking method.

Bemjag: An American seasoning that consist of a blend of brown sugar, red pepper, cumin, allspice, cinnamon, sage, thyme, marjoram, salt, fresh garlic and onion that will compliment all meat, fish and vegetable dishes.

Boiling: Foods submerged in water or stock at a temperature of 212 ° F.

Broth: Flavored extracted from fish, meat or vegetables by boiling.

Brunch: A meal which replaces both breakfast and lunch.

Brine: A mixture of water and other seasonings to preserve foods.

Cast iron cookware: Heavy and cumbersome. Distributes heat evenly. Special care should be imposed and kept thoroughly cleaned when cookware is cold and greased to prevent rust and pitting when immersed while hot in cold water.

Cheese cloth: A cotton mesh used to strain food.

China cap: A cone shape strainer.

Colander: A circular strainer with wire mesh.

Coffee liner: Designed for coffee grounds, improvised use as a home food strainer.

Crepe: A delicate griddle cake make with a very thin egg batter.

Cuisine: Foods that are made from scratch by various ethnicities.

Cure: A conglomerate of spices, herbs and brine to alternate texture.

Dough: A mixture of milk, flour and other ingredients.

Egg wash: A mixture of water, milk and egg.

Frying: A dry heat method by cooking with oil, sauteing or stir frying.

Game: Animals hunted in the wild for food and they are also raised domestically.

Grading: To appoint a food overall quality

Marinate: Soaking food for a certain time period to ensure tenderness.

Mince: To cut in small pieces.

Nopales: A prickly pear cactus native to Mexico and Southwestern United States, used a tasty vegetable.

Organic farming: A method that is void of pesticides, herbicides.

INDEX

Made in the USA
Middletown, DE
17 March 2022

62806391R00086